LOVE TALK

Volume 1

To put fire in your bosom—God's heart exposed

by

Scott E. Beemer

Black Forest Press
Mosheim, Tennessee
February 2006
First Edition

LOVE TALK

Volume 1

To put fire in your bosom—God's heart exposed

by

Scott E. Beemer

PUBLISHED IN THE UNITED STATES OF AMERICA
BY
BLACK FOREST PRESS
490 Mountain View Drive
Mosheim, TN 37818

Cover design
by
Aurora Zhivago

Scriptures are taken from the New King James Version, copyright 1979, 1982 by Thomas Nelson, Inc. Publishers. Used by permission.

Disclaimer

This document is an original work of the author. It may include reference to information commonly known or freely available to the general public. Any resemblance to his published information is purely coincidental. The author has in no way attempted to use material not of his own origination. Black Forest Press disclaims any association with or responsibility for the ideas, opinions or facts as expressed by the author of this book. No dialogue is totally accurate or precise.

Printed in the United States of America
Library of Congress
Catalogue-in-Publication

ISBN: 1-58275-170-6

ALL RIGHTS RESERVED

ACKNOWLEDGEMENTS

The Holy Spirit inspired this book.
It was received by both Scott Beemer
and Annetta Jean Beemer during
their morning devotions.

Thanks is given to my wife Annetta Jean Beemer
for her loving care, encouragement, and assistance
in writing this book.

DEDICATION

To God's Open Forum and the
San Diego First Assembly of God's
"Saints Alive Group."

PROLOGUE

The words of this book flow from the Heart of God to provide God's children the tools for their END TIME ADVANCEMENT. Think it not a strange thing that I come forth now in this Manner because this is the final gathering time for My Son's Bride, and I intend that He have only the finest and best of My Earth's children. Read My words here given and seek Me as you never have before, because I am extending wonderful courtesies of love at this time to all who believe and grow from what is here written. If you will prepare your heart I will open My heart and We will come to Our Oneness.

CONTENTS

THIS BOOK CONTAINS SHORT LESSONS FROM THE HEART OF GOD.

TO PROPERLY USE THEM YOU MAY READ ONE OR TWO AT A TIME, AS YOU ARE LED [USE AS A DAILY DEVOTIONAL].

OR YOU MAY OPEN THE BOOK ANYWHERE AT YOUR DISCRETION TO BE BLESSED.

THE GOAL

It is with great effort man overcomes self. The trying must be fully desired and God inspired. Ask and keep on asking, "Father help set me free from this self so I may fully receive Jesus in My heart." It is this slow purposeful seeking Jesus that is rewarded. This is the goal most desired. This is the path of All Spiritual blessings and only persistent efforts will attain to all that it implies. Here dear children are made plain the way of truth and light. No other seeking will be so precious, will be so worthwhile, and will be so well rewarded. So My dear ones read and believe, believe and receive. This is the way most pleasing to your Heavenly Father.

Almighty God shall lead the way. He has a plan for you and has sent to you the Holy Spirit to show the way. Listen to His still soft voice and know His will for you. Bury His word in your heart and mind that you may not falter. Focus your thoughts on Jesus and the word. Cast out all evil thoughts and worldly thoughts and replace them with God's word. Glory and have joy in being a child of God. Let His way and His love be your guiding star.

PERFECT PLACE

When the time is right, right things will happen. Try to see things in the same way I do. There are many children involved in My plan so I require cooperation from all to make My plan work to the perfection the Father calls for. See yourself as part of a large desire of God, then you can hold on waiting for culmination of His plan, not just the satisfying of your desire alone. Together blessings bring increase, alone there is a hold put on the flow of rewards. See yourself as a part of the whole work of God and then believe He has a perfect place just for you. Your believing is part of the stitching of a tapestry of love for all of His children. Proper love in each child will bring perfect peace in waiting. Waiting is an important part of testing. Rejoice and be happy with what you know you have, then you are prepared for what you don't know you already have that's about to be revealed. It is very important to keep minute-by-minute control so no slip-up is made. Be aware of your two enemies self and Satan.

"The effectual fervent prayer of a righteous man availith much." Have faith in God for He will answer your prayers. He hears the prayers of His children, He has the solution and His timing is perfect. God is faithful and His love covers all. Draw close to the Lord in prayer. Fill your heart with worship and praise and thanksgiving. Let the blood of Jesus cover your sins, knowing you are washed clean by His blood. Let your supplication for others come from your heart, knowing that all things are possible through Jesus Christ. Pray in the name of Jesus, your blessed advocate with God, and trust that He hears and answers.

CAREFUL ATTENTION

Sometimes it takes great effort to draw closer to Me because of all that surrounds you. There are more things effecting you than you are aware of, sounds, light, air all have a means of touching your spirit differently. My world is the world of the Spirit and I'm drawing you into a closer walk in the Spirit. This requires your more careful attention than you are giving it. Try to know My closeness, try to listen more during the day. All this draws you into a closer walk that is required for your task ahead. We have a plan unfolding, which means much to the Father. Keep aware and listening, yes write more down as you think about it!

"My grace is sufficient for you." God's grace is always more than sufficient. It is mixed with God's favor and His mighty love. What could be greater? Follow His commandment of love, love of the Father and love of others and you will always be covered by His grace and showered with His favor. Walk in His righteousness and reap a harvest of blessings. "Seek ye first the kingdom of God, and His righteousness, and all these things shall be added unto you." God will open the windows of heaven and pour out His blessings on you. Have faith in your Heavenly Father. He wants to bless you!

HIS DESIRES

It is your reaction to the events of the world, your small daily ones, and the rest of the world around you that will make or break you. Break self out of you or break you out of God's hand. This is necessary for the testing of your place with the Father. It's all about the Father and His desires, when this truth settles in your spirit then your opportunities will open. This path is one all must walk. The choosing is always going on and the purpose of this plan never changes. Each child of Mine must come to a life changing conclusion, will I truly let go of self and follow Jesus or will I dance around this decision until its to late? The whole-hearted release of self will come with such ease when you finally let go. Jesus is all you need and He will see you through. Church going, singing praises, doing a lot of nice things can be barriers keeping you from making this most important decision, "Give up self and follow Jesus." only what the Holy Spirit leads you to do counts, God will discard all of "your good works."

Enjoy Our companionship. Know that I am always with you. You may call upon Me at any time. You may ask of Me anything, and if it is of righteousness, I will supply it. I have a limitless supply of love, peace, and joy, patience, gentleness, faith, self-control, and meekness. All these blessings I can give to you. They are waiting to be released to your use. I am your comforter, and your helper. I would that you acknowledge My presence at all times. God has a beautiful plan for your life and I am to help you walk in that plan. Call on Me, dear one. Listen for My directions and My help and you will know the joy of the Lord.

ONE ROAD

When will My will be the only thing you do? Only when self is given back to Me. I gave it on loan to you until you made your choices leading back to Me. But now with that behind you, can't you let go completely? Say, "Father I return to you that "self" that drives Me and I reject it completely, now I can move on with your Holy Spirit because He is all I need. My connection with the Father is now complete and I am truly One. This is the walk I desire, "To be one with My God forevermore." I am never to stray, never to wander, never to leave, but just have Him by my side forever. All that I am is to be like Jesus, all that I desire is this wonderful blessing, to be just what He has called Me to be. There is only one way and one road ahead of Me that I must travel. My dear children when your road has brought you this far you are just where you need to be. The work is Mine and We are One, come walk with Me always.

Another day, God's gift to you, use it to the Glory of God. Walk uprightly in His will, always expecting the best. God's hand is upon you, His love surrounds you, and His peace fills your heart so let His joy bubble forth from your soul. Let joy reign in your life, a joy that others can see and feel. "The joy of the Lord is your strength." Continually say and know "All is well." That is your expression of trusting the Lord. For truly God is always in charge so "All is well."

LISTENING FOR INSTRUCTIONS

It is quickly becoming the time of the very end and you must start on the last leg of your journey. You can never get somewhere until you come from someplace, so you first must come to some place that prepares you to go to your everlasting place. Every trip requires you to pack and prepare, and then make arrangements for the journey. In your case most of this is already done, but you now have to prepare yourself. The discipline of time and the listening for instructions are now your necessary tasks.

In thy presence is fullness of joy. Still the busy body and the anxious soul and receive the peace and joy of His presence. Focus on Jesus and let the worldly cares fade away. Worship and praise Him for who He is, the Creator of this world, of all things including you. He created everything in love. Do not let the evil forces pollute His love. "Greater is He that is in you than he that is in the world." Call on that truth to reinforce your peace and joy. Bring this quiet spirit with you in all your relationships. Let it wash onto others in a flood of love and compassion. See Jesus in others and you will experience this love. The victory comes through God's great love!

LISTEN FOR HELP

The daily running after self-pleasing will soon draw you into a slippery pit. Keep your eyes on things of the Spirit, ask, seek, and listen for My help. I can vary your day in many fruitful ways, but you must listen carefully to bring My help to your benefit. Keep in mind I always have you under careful watch. Knowing this should slow you down and cause you to ponder your way. Our walk should always be where I lead you. Can you look back and say that has been so? No one is perfect but I will never stop drawing you there! Do you always need something new and exciting to keep you going? That should not be, am I not exciting enough for you?

Speak the name of Jesus often. The word tells you to pray in the name of Jesus. That Holy Name is your authority over evil. As children of God you are joint-heirs with Jesus, therefore you can do all things. Remember, "I can do all things through Christ who strengthens me." Your connection with Jesus, your redeemer, is the answer. He is the connection, and the power, and love of God. Through Him all things are possible. Let the love of Jesus, the name of Jesus be your banner over all things.

CONSTANT DESIRE

There is never a good time or a bad time to seek Me, any time, any where is just the right environment for making a lost child safe with Me. This is My constant desire to bring all of the lost children home safe with Me. You who know this, you who have answered My call and have come into My arms now have the last opportunity to save lost children of Mine. Not for them alone do I make this plea, because in your obedience you will open up a window of opportunity through which I can bless you with great blessings you know not of. Test Me, try Me, and just see if this is so! I have store houses of rewards and blessings you know not of, because you ask not nor do you try to find out these things, but your time to obey and know is fast fading away so I bring this word that it may fall on obedient ears and hearts that will respond. Will you now move on My request?

Have patience and persevere in doing God's will. His ways are not your ways and His time is not your time. Let your faith cover every situation knowing that God is in charge. His will for you is Spiritual growth so learn the lessons that come your way. Be aware of what needs to be corrected in your life and let God help you change. Trust His loving care to make the changes necessary. Submit to the lessons you are experiencing and let God's correction have its way. Trust and obey is your solution. In this attitude peace will come upon you and you can be led by the Holy Spirit rather than self. Walk gently in love, expecting the lessons to come, then be ready to be victorious because the Lord is in charge. His Glory makes all things possible.

I TEST

When I give directions I expect them to be adhered to, do so by listening with all of your heart, then hear with your ears. My word will come as I please, so it is your place to always listen. Be My ready one, so to stand by is to be obedient. I speak to your heart not your head, hear Me rightly inside, and then move on the outside. Only My chosen ones are so directed, therefore I test them more than others. Do not make judgments that you know not of. Keep your eyes on Our actions, and that will be more than enough to occupy you. Just know and have confidence about your place and position, only then can I use you. Slowly I will hastily move to keep the Father's planned perfect place.

Trust that whatever you need will be provided. "My God shall supply all your needs according to His riches in Glory by Jesus Christ." Your loving Heavenly Father knows what you need and what your heart desires. He is faithful and just to provide. In His love He also will provide the lessons necessary for your Spiritual growth. Walk through each day confident that you are learning and growing, and that God has His hand on you. With Jesus as your advocate in heaven God sees you perfected. Walk confident that His abiding love is always with you.

ONGOING PLAN

The continued writing will be put to use so don't give up. I have an ongoing plan of worth for obedience. Just keep close to Me because We will be embarking on a journey of love to places in need. Keep drawing closer all the time because I can use your talent and help. Yes, I depend on My children; it is My main way of pleasing the Father. Keep trust high and listen more carefully. Do not fear, have no regrets, keep on course and listening.

What you see as trials and tribulations are really lessons to be learned on the path of life. You do not stay in problems and difficulties but you go through them. Remember, "Yea though I walk through the valley of shadow of death, I shall fear no evil, for thou art with me." I go through all things with you and if necessary I will carry you through. But are you learning the lessons presented or will you have to experience this lesson again? Persevere, My child, and have faith. All is well, I am in charge and you are growing Spiritually. Look toward the future, be confident in Our Oneness. Let My presence be your power and guide. Have joy in Our togetherness!

A NEW TRAIL

When We have finished one work, then We are able to open new doors and walk through new corridors. Come let Us take a new trail to seek and find the things the Heavenly Father has set in Our path. Open eyes will bring new heart joy and peace, because seeing is the door opening into new places. Where each day takes you will depend on the acceptance of your days past. Our walk can only be taken when past trails have led to plateaus of revelation accepted and welcomed. Knowledge is one thing, but to have understanding revealing knowledge's sources is another level of revelation. Our walk will be in new fields that are as yet unplowed. Revelation knowledge will bring with it paths of joy and works of difficulty. But just as cliffs climbed bring views of spectacular beauty so can eyes open to Spirit revelation show new wonders. I desired My children to have new glimpses of My places of work that they may expand their thinking. We must keep the picture God wants revealed clear enough that comprehension flows willingly.

Despite the pull of the earth, and the influence of worldly things, My Glory is greater. It is an influence of light and righteousness. My presence brings the strength, peace, patience, and Godly wisdom necessary for any task, for every situation. Let Us commune together in love. Quietly draw from My strength. "They that wait upon the Lord shall renew their strength." Be ye renewed, let the new man within penetrate to the soul and body and bring righteous vigor to your life. My children, I am here for you. Draw on Me and live abundantly.

ATTENTION

When time is pressing never let it press you out of My will. Keep a clear and open channel at all times for Our work to proceed. My call on each child's life is a forever one and passing actions of earth's making should have little effect on and no influence in Our togetherness. Keep this note in mind My dear children because of the immediate times pending. Attention, all of your attention should now turn to My plans and Me and desires for each of you. Yes, My plans for each of you will continue to unfold and it is to your advantage to flow with them. Spend more time with Me now for all your eternity will be blessed by your obedience.

Walk uprightly in His love, in a quiet and peaceful spirit, and when you have a need ask for it. The word says, "You have not because you ask not." God has a bountiful supply of everything you may need. Ask in the name of Jesus, believing that you receive it, and it shall be given unto you. God is love and His desire is that His children should have life and that more abundantly. It is necessary that you grow in the Spirit, so persevere in the things God would have you do. Learn the lessons that are before you. Be an over-comer knowing that God is always with you supplying strength, wisdom, and love. He will make a way if you lean on Him. "They that wait upon the Lord shall renew their strength." Be renewed today in My love.

DESIRE HIM

The failure of men to clearly see truth is because God carefully guards His plan of salvation for those who truly desire Him. The only hearts to be saved are truth seeking, God desires the ones that choose life out of love for Him. No man comes to the Father unless the Holy Spirit draws him. The sincere prayer of a righteous man saves men with the Holy Spirit drawing them. It is God who knows men's hearts and God who chooses; so men choose life by God's drawing love. Pray for the salvation of My lost children, come team up with Us and We can save many of My lost ones!

Blessed be My children who walk in My ways. My ways are not a mystery; they are made clear in My word. I have given you the Holy Spirit to indwell you, to help you, to comfort and guide you. Listen to His still soft voice, as it is My voice, My directions, and My will for your life. Be a willing vessel for My plan is wonderful and filled with blessings. Go willingly from one level of Spiritual growth to another. Have confidence that, "You can do all things through Christ who strengthens you." We are a team, I am the leader and I supply everything necessary for your walk here on earth. We are One!

TRY AND SEE

The pattern of man's loss of fellowship with God is very simply the pleasing of self first and foremost. Until God comes first man is lost. Only I am to be the leader. Only I am the King, only I have the truth and the way. Why does man not see the obvious? Oh My children only by facing your puny position and life on this earth and admitting the truth of My creation will I ever be able to set you truly free with Me. Come dear ones draw closer every moment you have left and know Me in truth and reality. Listen for My still sincere voice within, obey and be led by My Spirit I put within My obedient ones and I will show purpose to your life and bring knowledge setting you free from all your failures. My way can be made true today as you obey. Try Me and see!

"Greater is He that is in you than he that is in the world." Remember My promise to you when you grow weary. Look to your Heavenly Father for strength and guidance. Let the joy of the Lord fill your soul and renew your strength. Renew your faith daily by praise and thanksgiving. Count your many blessings and remember how the Lord has always been faithful in the past. Praise Him constantly for, "The Lord inhabits the praises of His people."

My children look up and know that help is always available. Step out in confidence that My love and blessings are enfolding you. Acknowledge Me, call on Me, and rest in Me, for I truly am your source. You have the victory!

KEEP ME FOREMOST

The constant attention to My desires brings a heart felt loving response from Me every time. My dear children, always keep Me foremost in your thoughts and plans, this way allows My continued care and protection over you to be shown as worth maximum efficiency. We are in all things together anyway, so you should take advantage of the best way for Us to work together. To know the best way to go and use it will prove to be a great blessing lasting through "always". Each simple instruction I give, that you obey, is building a sure place of great worth forever. I'm making this point now so all who read or hear this message will find blessings of great value flowing in their life from now on.

SHIELD OF PEACE

Following the lead I give will never fail you. Your obedience builds a wall of protection and brings every help when needed. To be open and willing to receive the things I desire is a shield of peace and comfort to My children, not only to the obedient one but also to all they encounter. Never doubt the spread of My influence when coming through an obedient channel. All of these little hints and notes are not for your guiding only, but they are for everyone who reads them. I speak and it is to all of My children, and it will come at just the right time, the right place, and for the right purpose.

God's gracious love makes all things possible. His perfect peace flowing through your life is the oil that smoothes the way. Let the Lord have His way in your daily walk. "Trust in the Lord with all your heart, lean not on your own understanding in all your ways acknowledge Him and He will direct your path. "Let these words of scripture be your guiding light and the Lord will shower you with His blessings. Allow your faith to grow, always knowing that He is in charge and you are His creature, His child. Let His perfect plan be fulfilled in your life.

GIFT FOREVERMORE

When time runs out where will you be, do you know, are you sure? Every child of Mine should know, they should answer with a loud positive YES! I WILL BE WITH JESUS! Oh what a joy released, a joy like nothing man can know, only My children will have this gift forevermore. To know My joy is to be filled with loves release absorbing, all each one can take of peace and well-being. Keep this picture on your heart, through night and day until truth is released as only the Father can do. Become filled with this certainty of truth, because as you believe so you will receive. Yes even here and now My joy can penetrate the cares of this old world and release a measure of My joy. I am always ready to help, always ready to lead and guide My willing ones on this trip. When are you ready?

Let your faith carry you through the day, confidently trusting the Lord to be your strength, your joy and your loving leader. He is able to supply all your needs and do so abundantly. Jesus said, "I have come that they may have life and that more abundantly. "Live life abundantly, and walk in what Jesus has prepared for you. Do not let His great sacrifice be in vain. Claim all the blessings Jesus has made possible for you. Look toward the time of Oneness with Jesus and Almighty God, your Heavenly Father. See yourself covered with the Glory and love He has for His child. Be an active part of the family of God. He has prepared a special place for you in the body of Christ. As you step out confidently, He will supply all that is needed. Trust and obey and His love will carry you through.

LOVE

It is with great regret that I tell some of My children My truth, because their reaction will cause them to lose Me. Free will will cause My greatest sorrow, but the price I pay is as the Father demands. The saved children are the harvest so dear. I must always turn to the source of the Father's greatest joy "Love." In all of Our Universe there will never be a gift so great as Our gift of everlasting love! What makes a gift so precious? Only the gift giver can ever answer all the truth behind that question. Where is this source of love We speak about? What fountain pours forth love forever? Where does love come from, when does it go? My dear children seek love, cry for it, work for it, call out for it and you will know it's been there all of the time!

Seek truth always; search the word for God's truth and direction in your life. Let His words be your guide and you will eliminate much strife and conflict. Let His peace be the balm that smoothes out the difficult situations. Walk in this earthly realm knowing to whom you belong. Always remember God's love is around about you. It is your protection, your peace, your guide, and even your strength. "The joy of the Lord is My strength." Move slowly into new situations, stop and listen for directions from your Comforter, the Holy Spirit. He is God's gift to you. Acknowledge Him and He will direct your path. Walk in victory!

WHAT WORTH?

When I call a man he should respond with total acceptance and attention, but many are his distractions. It is the handling of this life activity that allows Me to see just what worth I can make of each child of Mine. My desire is for all of his attention and his self-desire is just the opposite, so in this tug of love I have the testing tool of decision. The release of this knowledge is a great "Decision Requirer." Now you who read this have a life changing challenge, what will you do now that you are confronted with My will and way? Will you just set and wait for Me to give you your next move or will you decide to just please self and wait and see what happens? Perhaps you will give Me a little more time and attention once in a while? Just maybe I can have an hour or two each day? What will be your time set-aside just for Us?

Walk in the light as He is in the light, He is light, gloriously showing the way. His ways are not a mystery. If you stay close to your loving Heavenly Father His light will show you the way, His perfect will for you. "God is light, and in Him is no darkness at all." Trust in Him to show the way. Have a submissive heart and let God and His word lead the way. "Thy word is a lamp unto my feet, and a light unto my path." His plan for you is one of Spiritual growth so you can one day be one with the Lord. Put self behind you and let the lord lead the way. He would that you have life and that more abundantly. Let your faith grow and live in that victorious life.

WALK AS IF

There is no blessing like the blessings given to My obedient ones. To know this is true is to be "The Anointed of the Lord." Pray for, then walk as if, and you who are true will know! My dear ones never take the words I give without testing them in your hearts. In this manner you will have the blessings of truth revealed. Only My true ones are so anointed that they may receive blessings beyond the knowledge of all. Yes it is true, blessings I give are released only to proper receptacles, how else should they be given? Only true listeners are the available servants of My word. All children are saved, but all do not know the fullness of My desires for them. I delight in open hearts with open ears and hands eager to be used, so guide your walk to make it a walk of wisdom bringing forth blessed obedience!

Are you learning the lessons the Lord has prepared for you today? Are thoughts of Jesus uppermost in your thinking? Is your mind full of thanksgiving and praise for your loving Heavenly Father? You are what you think. My children think about what you are thinking about. Let your thoughts and your words glorify God. "Let the words of my mouth and the meditations of my heart be acceptable in thy sight, Oh Lord my strength and my redeemer." Think before you speak, think before you act. Will this glorify the Lord? Think about your motives and let them be pleasing to your blessed Heavenly Father.

LOSE SELF

Man's expressions of love are so far from the real love I give. My love is everlasting and eternal through all of everything. Come My dear ones and know Me by My love. Your release of self-pleasing, self-serving, and just selfishness will help break forth the outpouring of My love in such a way that man can't contain it. I must control this release, but I must have ready and willing receptacles of worth. To be worthy is to lose self; to lose self properly is to be like Jesus. Jesus is to be all in all for My family to know the trueness of love. The trueness of My love must begin in man's heart by choice, so dear ones, knowing this is your clue to the wonders of heaven released.

My children should face each day with expectation and excitement. Ask yourself what will the Lord do today in my life? What lessons can I learn that will bring about the Spiritual growth I need to walk closer to Jesus? Who can I show love to, the love of Jesus? What need can I fill for the Lord? Walk confidently knowing that I am with you. My strength is your strength; My joy your joy. Listen quietly for directions from the Holy Spirit. For the word says, "For as many as are led by the Spirit of God they are the sons of God." His way is perfect for you. Let Him lead you on a victorious path every day closer to your loving Heavenly Father.

COMPLETE ACCESS

It is the continually pursuing of My will and way that opens up man's understanding of all I have written in My Bible. I have not left My children bereft, without recourse, and alone to find a way into My Kingdom, but I have provided full recourse and opportunity for each and every one of them to have complete access to everything I have given to My adopted Son Jesus. My love of My children is just the same as My love for Jesus. He has set the path of victory for every seeker.

He has adequately and perfectly accomplished all that I required and asked of Him; therefore My expectation is for every child that hears, reads, is shown and told about Him, will come into My arms in true believing. Those who accept and know Him must be a teller of all He has done. As obedience is displayed I will release further knowledge to be shown. No one is left short of works to be done for Me.

OUR ONENESS

When I call someone they are to be changed as never before. When I call someone they are to change their life so it becomes My life in them, through them, and by them. I am to live in the life of each child of Mine because the Father has set all men to obtain Our Oneness and it only comes with Our totalness. Open your arms to Me so I may enter your heart. Your heart is the center of Our being. Our being with you forever, Our being One with you always, Our being becomes Our Oneness. Can you not yet see the plan of eternity unfolding in these words I bring? Do you not comprehend the journey you are on, the one I have called you to? Still your own desires, it is My desires that inspires! Come dear Ones see as I see, feel as I feel, love as I love, this is the Father's Oneness you are called to.

Still the body, quiet the mind and soul, loose the Holy Spirit to bring My thoughts to you. The Holy Spirit is the mind of Christ as well as your comforter, so take advantage of My gift to you. My children you must be led by the Holy Spirit. All solutions to every problem come from that source, He is within you and available to you. Let that peace that He supplies flood your soul and body. Let His love do a work in your life. Claim the fruit of the Spirit: love, peace, joy, patience, meekness, self-control and faith. These are God's gifts to you through the Holy Spirit. Live your life with God's power working through you. Truly be a joint-heir with Jesus!

WHO IS LEFT BEHIND?

It is My task to continually call and seek to inspire My loved ones. It is seldom they respond with consistency and purpose to serve. To each one who hears, and understands, with the desire to pursue to victory, I can find great pleasure in their obedience. Come dear ones, come and draw closer to Me in the short time left. Don't you know how late it is, and how soon I must take you all away, and don't you care who's left behind? Listen and I will tell you your part, and then you can embark upon a trip that will open the windows of heaven to others and to yourself. Just think about what's implied in what I just said! I will help you draw the lost children into the place prepared for them thus fulfilling the Father's plan. Have you earned your PHD? [Planned Heavenly Departure]

In a calm spirit God's love is released. In total trust there is no agitation, only peace and a quiet spirit ready to hear from the Lord. Trust and obey and the will of God will be fulfilled. Walk confidently in faith knowing that God's bubble of love and peace is about you. If the Holy Spirit is your guide you can step out boldly. Be constantly joyful with a heart full of thanksgiving. Let others see that Christians have the joy of the Lord. Truly the, "Joy of the Lord is your strength!"

MAKE NOTE

When will all of My plans for My children start to be so obvious that the unsaved will notice? Not until My called ones release it. Yes, you who hear and obey are the door of opening to the end of this phase of God's time of drawing all men unto Himself. Make note of this word because judgment is involved in it. I will cause the release of the church to come home when the church finds the freedom of obedience to motivate that completion. All time hangs on My children's proper moves and motivations. Yes, I am in charge and I have set the time, but this is how it is set! I am also watching love's path growing, this being the key to all unfolding joy. Stir up love in everyone you meet and watch the opposition tumble.

Lift up your head and walk in your blessings and inheritance. You are a child of God, joint-heirs with Jesus! Your Father, Almighty God created you to be a part of His family. Be that son or daughter; receive the wonderful blessings He has for you. Walk in the light, His light, for it is available to you. There is no darkness in Him. Do not allow the darkness in your life. If it creeps in, cast it out by using the Scriptures in the Name of Jesus. Rise above the worldly cares and problems by focusing on your Savior.

QUICK VICTORY

It is the dwelling with Me in Spirit that drives out all opposition to the Father's plan. If My people will knowingly, with purpose, do My will each day, then I can draw out the Family of My choice. The time is such that obedience must now be called for. If you are one of My called ones then you hear My voice. If what you read here is what My voice is saying to you then how long will you resist? Complete satisfaction awaits all who hear and obey. Come now dear ones didn't you always know this time must come, why do you hesitate? Reluctance dissipates rewards and blessings. Take charge now of your unwilling ways and turn them to quick victory with Me.

Go slowly, there is always enough time to do My will. Walk always in love, My love. Let others see the love of the Lord in you, My children. Remember, "All is well" so reflect this to whomever you see. When you see a need, fill it if possible. I will supply all things necessary to have My love and My will spread abroad. I am your source and you should look to Me for strength and wisdom. As you walk in My will, peace and joy will follow, and surely you will say, "All is well."

WORK TOGETHER

The opening of man's understanding will come only as We as a team do the work together. You release I fill in. This is a taking out and putting in. You take out man's old self; I put in more of Jesus. All growth in the Spirit is so produced. You let go I fill in. By this symphony of cooperation a planned place is prepared for Jesus to fill all in all. Only by this method will children grow into the beautiful outlet of love I have planned for them. Truly God's plan is all encompassing and all complete, equipping the children for the eternal walk the Father has set for them. Rejoice in perfection because you, His children, are surrounded and protected by it in every way. You are the choice children of a loving Father, FOREVER!

My children wait upon the Lord and you shall renew your strength. The worldly way is to hurry, I say go-slow. Keep your eyes on Me and let My peace enfold you and direct you. My ways are not your ways. But My ways lead to peace and to heaven for a forever life with Me. There is joy in My way and an abundant life. Let go of the secular business and walk with Me in love.

SELF-DECEPTION

Is there anywhere I can't take you, is there anywhere We can't go? Why would I say that unless I had a purpose? I desire your "Totalness" all of you, all of the time, anyplace and anywhere and in any situation. When will you release "self" and submit all your time to Me? Do you think I will suddenly whisk you away somewhere you don't want to go? Why are you reluctant to trust Me completely? What a barrier this reluctance is to Our walking always together, everywhere. Come My dear ones can't you see through this self-deception? It is time, NOW for your complete change! Don't put off this wonderful step of faith into My arms.

Lean upon the Lord and know that He is making a way for you. Put all things in His hands for His plan is perfect. The work that He began, He will finish. Before beginning a work be in prayer, and listen for the directions from the Holy Spirit. Be sure that self is not leading the way. Take into your heart and soul more of Jesus. As Jesus fills your being, self is diminished. Do this in prayer, in praise, in worship, in thanksgiving, and in blessing others. Truly I say to you, "Seek ye first the kingdom of God and His righteousness; and all these things shall be added unto you." Let His power, and His righteousness, be your strength and guide, and you will always walk in victory.

WALK OF FAITH

Listen more intently, listen at all times, never fail to hear My call to you and We will walk great paths together. It is in the hearing and obeying that I draw you into your final walk of faith. There is a time coming when My called ones will be as I am. The Father lives in My heart and I walk with him all of the time. My children you should hear and answer readily, to be able to respond to Me readily, for I am your path of preparation making you ready soil for the Father's purposes forever. What a gift, what a wonder, what a life of purpose that is for all of the Family of God. Make this your forever goal, to know the Father and be His forever in will and way. You will learn to walk the path of love throughout eternity! Make God's purposes your purposes!

I know you as only the Creator can know His creation. I fashioned you to be unique and special, to minister to My lost and hurting ones. I understand you and have compassion on you always. My love is your hedge and protection against trials, and your strength during the weak times. My love allows you to be an over-comer and to rise above the evils of the world. Stay always under that covering of love. Let Jesus fill your soul and mind, that you truly may have the mind of Christ. It is possible as you are joint-heirs with the Lord Jesus. My children claim your blessings and walk in love. Rest in My Love always!

CHANGE YOUR WAYS

The everlasting life I offer will come to all who I call, but the kind of life they receive will have a lot to do with what they do with My gifts that I offer to them. You see dear ones We are in this eternal life together but I have one place and you will have your place, just where the Father allows and puts you. Your place then is dependent upon how the Father views your heart for Him and His desires. Are you fulfilling your desires all the time now? If so that is not a good habit to bring into your Father's house. Change your ways now to receive My rewards and blessings that will be allowed by Our Father. No one makes his own way, God's way is now open to all who listen, hears, and does! Be wise, this time is given to be used to your best advantage by you.

God in His tender mercy and great love for His children has provided a way. He has given you the Holy Spirit to indwell you, to lead and guide, to comfort and be your helper. The pull of the world is great but, "Greater is He that is in you than he that is in the world." All God's blessings are available within you. The fruit of the Spirit is released when you call upon Him. Acknowledge the great gift of love God has given you, and make it an active part of your life. More love of God, more of Jesus in your heart releases the blessings within. In this way self is decreased and the Lord Jesus increased in your life. Let His love be the light of your life and walk in the joy of the Lord forever.

A SURE LOVE

The call I call has been put out to all of My children, not one call, but I call and I call. Why would that be so, just because I have not made it easy. The Father requires a "sure love" to be shown from all those to be saved, so I call and I call. Isn't it a shame that I must be doing this so much? Why aren't My children listening and eager for My call? This earth time is given as a place of testing, and tests will be given. The Father requires "true love" from His children, and only over-comers prove true love. So dear ones "Be over-comers" in all the time you have left. Believe Me, your time is very short. Only God's purpose served will be proof of God's love indwelling.

"Seek Ye first the kingdom of God and His righteousness, and all these things shall be added unto you." My children remember My words to you. The things of God and His righteousness are forever. The things of the world are so temporary and do not fulfill or bring joy. By walking in My righteousness I can give you more love, peace and joy. I will truly lift you up to heavenly places and fill your heart with the joy of the Lord. You are in control, and you choose what kind of a life you will live. Walk with Me in the light and experience My love, or seek after the world and things of darkness. I love you My child. Let My love cover you with blessings all the days of your life. Live life abundantly!

TRUTH FLOWING

When I write down My thoughts and desires I expect the written word to be read and passed on, to never stop until all have read, heard or experienced the truth of My word. All My word is truth no matter the source through which I bring it. It is truth flowing that matters. Truth is the picture given through which I build My desires. I am truth, My thoughts are truth, and I create truth and will always prove My truth. Truth is exposing Me in various ways I desire to be shown. All truth is never in one place because I am everywhere therefore all truth is never seen. I expand and flow in and through My truth and send it anywhere I desire. Seek truth and I will appear, tell truth and I know, walk in truth and you'll find I am leading. Seek truth and you'll be surprised at My disclosures. All truth seekers find! All truth seekers I draw. Be a truth seeker and your growth will never end!

There is power in the name of Jesus. Everything in this world and beyond must bow to the name of Jesus. You have been given this name to call upon for strength, for wisdom, and for direction. You are joint-heirs with Jesus and are growing into this Spiritual awareness. Trust God's word that teaches your authority with Jesus because of His love and sacrifice. The word says, "Ask anything in My name and you shall receive it if you believe," trust in that name, trust in the word. Lean on your loving Heavenly Father for He cares for you and will renew your strength. Jesus made a way for you. Do not let it be in vain. His love conquers all. Open your heart to Him and receive all He has for you. This will bring the victory in your life.

DEEPER TRUTH

Listen to truth when it is spoken, seek the truth behind the obvious, never just accept truth on face value because a true truth seeker will always pursue truth until My end of truth is known. Hear, see, reach for, and feel in your Spirit My truth, and then I can set you free to follow a closer walk with Me. No real truth is simple because I am not simple. There are many facets and depths to real truth. Obvious truth is given only to entice and draw you into deeper truth. Deeper truth is then found in a closer walk with Me. Only I can release all truth, but only as the Father gives permission. Never doubt the closeness We all have in truth. Come be a truth seeker as you answer My call on your heart. Walk the path of "glowing wonder," this is where all truth leads. My Glory opens hearts to wonderful truths of Glory in the Father and all of His works. Come follow the Father's call on His children's heart.

All is well! All is well because Jesus takes your cares and burdens. All is well because Jesus made a way for you to go boldly to the throne of God. All is well because you have the precious gift of salvation and the Holy Spirit dwelling within. When problems arise learn the lessons they present. These are opportunities for Spiritual growth. Know that the Lord is with you, holding you up. He is your strength and your peace. Truly "You can do all things through Christ who strengthens you." Have the peace that comes from knowing, "All is well."

MOST SPECIAL TIME

It is the daily trials that will reward a man, when he overcomes them with Me. It is Our walk that deserves attention, all of the time, not the task or troubles right before him. Keep Me closer now than ever before because your benefits forever are depending on your moves now, in these times. I did not make this end time just to gather a family NO, it has much greater purpose than that. It is a "Most special time," because of the most special purposes being served. Just stop and consider what this "catching away" is. It is the Father's greatest desire and dream coming to pass. It is the greatest effort God has ever made; never before and never again, will a family in Our image and likeness be made. This gathering is "the most meaningful work of God. Give proper honor and consideration to it. Just stop and dwell on the wonder of it all. Millions of God's children meeting in the air and suddenly they are all like Jesus! Open your eyes to truth revealed!

As a child of God receive the grace and mercy He has for you. In His great love He has spread abroad His mercy and His peace. Walk in the blessings, trust and rely on the goodness of the Lord. Remember, "He which hath begun a good work in you will perform it until the day of Jesus Christ," Let patience rest in your soul as you trust the Lord to do all things right. Wait upon the Lord; He is working on your behalf. Learn the lessons before you, each one is important in your Spiritual growth, God sees the big picture and is putting all the pieces together in perfect order. The end is victory. Persevere!

LACK OF LOVE

The difficulty My children have in following Me all of the time is basically lack of love! Yes there are many kinds of love My children show, and all love starts from Me, but My love is contaminated by the self-rule of man. My children, those who truly love Me, cast all of their cares on Me. This allows My love open and complete access to flow unrestrained. But how many of My children can maintain My free love flowing? Here dear ones is a lesson of worth forever, Kill Self and receive all of Me, Jesus, then learn to keep Me as your guide and lover. This task when accomplished in you NOW, in this time, will release your "forever place" early and give you great advantage in Spiritual growth in Our kingdom. Come dear ones, hear this word of loving kindness and reap your harvest of love from the Father.

God's great love for you is an all-encompassing force that can change your life. Because God is love, His love is available to all. In love He sent His Son to make a way for you to be redeemed; He gifted you with the Holy Spirit; He sent His word to guide you through this earthly life. This "love force" is mighty and can bring God's peace and joy into your being. Acknowledge the Father and His Son Jesus Christ in your life. Let their love be your guiding light. You can only love others through Their marvelous love. Receive and show forth God's great gift of love.

JOY OF COMPLETION

If every child of Mine were truly Mine in their heart and soul they would still have to take the full time of My plan to come to Me. I have lessons and blessings, trials and testings that will develop My loved ones in just the right manner so they will become all that they need to be to fill Our hearts with satisfaction and joy of completion. Yes there is a course to run, and walk it We all must do, just to make full the heart of the Father. No "quick fixes," no sudden elevations, just the walk of planned perfection will complete God's Family. "All is well," repeat that often My dear ones because it shows your position with the Father and your trust in Him.

My children, always have an attitude of joy and anticipation. When you are trusting in the Lord all things are possible. Expect wonderful things to happen to you. Anticipate each day, knowing Jesus is beside you and His love conquers every foe. Walk humbly submitted to your God, but boldly knowing you are a child of a loving God and joint-heirs with His Son, Jesus. Always keep His presence about you and within you. He will guide, protect, and love you as a mother does her child.

WARNING TOLD

There are to be no more false tales told by My ministers! There are to be no more wrong lessons given to My Bride! I am bringing a stop to teaching that has no value, just talk. My children are dying for lack of knowledge and My teachers must take the stand for truth and righteousness. Everyone who tells tales of My word had better look to his heart for truth, and find it, or he better not talk. I will watch out for all My children, they need and deserve truth that leads, guides, and uplifts them. See, all of you who read this word, that you spread this warning and follow up on these words because I will watch over this note to see it properly accomplished!

Being obedient to the Lord is the result of faith. If you trust in the Lord you know all of His directions flow out of love for you. He will not ask you to do anything that is impossible. "You can do all things through Christ who strengthens you." Trust in His scriptures to you. "The work that He began in you, He will perform until the day of Jesus Christ." Call upon Me, the Holy Spirit and I can release the blessings stored up for you. Acknowledge the power and knowledge of the Godhead. It is there for the benefit of the family of God. You are a child of God. Submit to your Heavenly Father and receive His joy and peace. He will make all things possible.

TELL THEM

All of the time and effort man puts in to please himself will fade away as if it never happened. Every child of Mine should be telling everyone who doesn't know Me about Our relationship. You say but they don't listen or care! But I say, "Tell Them." I can only move in conjunction with what My children do, remember We are together in this work. You pray, I act and answer. You tell the lost about Me and I bring believing happenings to them. Only together will We do the work the Father has called Us to do. In teamwork comes victory. In going on your own only comes defeat. Wake up to these simple facts and make a perfect end to this work of Ours!

Trust and obey for that is the way to a closer walk with Jesus. Have faith in the word and the promises God has given you. Receive the blessings stored up for you and walk in them releasing God's love. Let peace lead the way, for when there is peace God's directions can follow. Have the peace He promised. "My peace I give you, not as the world gives, give I you. Let not your heart be troubled, neither let it be afraid." As you walk in His peace, faith will grow and you will be able to trust your Heavenly Father in all things.

ASKING ME

I am always ready to help you never doubt that, but you are the motivator, you are the source or beginning of all We can do together. How will you know this? Well just sit down and do nothing, your Holy Spirit is right there doing nothing with you. When will you start something? You can always start by asking Me what We should do. Have you ever asked? You start, I will move in answer and or in conjunction with you. First a desire, an idea, an object to pursue, then next a plan, a purpose laid out, and a start is made. You moving, then your Holy Spirit can lead, guide, and support you. Come dear ones let Us work together. How about just witnessing to one person today?

"Be still and know that I am God." In the stillness I can speak to you. As you quiet your soul and dwell on the Lord I am released. I am closer than your breath. I live within you to be your helper, your comforter, and to show you the way. You are My only concern and God's love is with Me to release to you. Oh My child, acknowledge the Almighty God within you, a gift in the form of the Holy Spirit. Live by the Spirit, and not by the flesh, and the earthly ways. Joy comes from a Spirit walk with Me.

BE WINNERS

If ever there was a perfect time for all My children to draw closer and love one another and love Me it is NOW. Now is the time of final release, release of gifts to bless, teach, and show My ways to all who will listen, heed, and do! Yes you who will do, rise up and prove your worth to Me and be winners by doing. All doing is self-released to be Spirit led. All doing is My doing through you. Watch and see how wonderful the results are. Yes you will see results, see healings, salvations, love, joy, and peace released and spreading, flowing like will-fire. Everyone will know and seize the freedom of love flowing!

My children have the mind of Jesus. Focus your thinking on the Lord and His word. What would He have you do? He would have you love God, serve the Lord and others, be a channel of blessings to all. Encompass the whole world in your prayer life. Open your thinking to include all of God's children. Where there is darkness, could your prayers bring in a bit of God's light? Reach out to a dying world in love and prayer. All are the children of your Heavenly Father and He would that all be saved. Be an active part of the Family of God.

WAKE UP

The working of My plan for you takes all of your time, because I am giving you all of My time. I live right inside of you. I am with you in everything you are doing, whether it is for Me or against Me. You can never hide from Me. You can always disregard Me, but you can never lose Me if you love Me. My love will sustain you, guide you, and build you up. Your disregard of Me will cause you great loss. You may not see or know this now, but your time of deep regret will come. Wake-up and make your time a time of great attainment, love, and adventure. I am always ready to take you on a journey of love. Believe, receive, and let's start all over again, making this day your beginning of a whole new walk.

Prepare yourself for the catching away. Help others to ready their hearts and souls for the coming of the Lord. This time, as you know it is fast coming to an end. Jesus is coming for His Bride soon. It is His heart's desire that all men know Him and accept Him as their Lord and Savior. His heart's desire is for you to spread the word and His love to all. He would that none be left behind. Can you, as His children, show forth His love and mercy to everyone you meet? Can you be in constant prayer for the souls of the unsaved children? What can you do today to prepare for the great "gathering" of the Lord? Let the joy of the Lord lead the way as you work for your Heavenly Father.

PATH OF WORTH

To be continuous in My work will prove to be well worth all the time and effort it has taken. Persistence is a building of a love path that only grows in benefit. Never stop; never consider any other course than the one I bring to you. All paths do not lead to the right place for those who are Mine. Only consistent attention and care to the things I bring to you will be your path from now on. Think of the service given to you as only a path of worth to be taken because of loves call. All the efforts given to My work will pay back in never ending ways. I will distribute as I see fit all of the rewards and blessings because they carry more and more responsibilities and purposes that are pleasing to the Father. Always keep your eyes on the path I have given you and all ways will prove of great value over and over again.

You are in charge, you speak the words and the body responds. You speak positive words, words of health and God's goodness and I, the Holy Spirit, can act upon them, as does your body. You speak negative words, the body hears, and decides it must be true. Words are powerful, they are creative. What are you creating by the words of your mouth? Know My word, know My will for your life and speak it. "Let the words of My mouth and the meditations of My heart be acceptable in your sight, oh Lord my strength and my redeemer." Remember all is well. Jesus came that you may have life and that more abundantly. Create that abundant life by the words of your mouth.

THE FATHER'S PLAN

The continuing task that I give you will never change, alter, or go in another direction. I chose you for a purpose; you are My friend, brother, and confidant. We are joint-heirs together before the Father. All that I lead you to do is from the Father. One purpose, united in love, never-ending, always in love, that is Our way forever. Come, receive, and believe, because Our way is God's desire. Dedication, obedience, persistence with a loving response will pave a victory path ordained by Our Father. Total dedication will find total rewards and blessings, not just for you but many are the children in your path waiting for their blessings to unfold. Come let Us go now hand in hand, heart with heart, and see eternal life unfolding, always in love, by love, and through love.

Let the words of your mouth be of praise and worship. Fill this day with praise and thoughts of the Lord and He will make a way for you. Leave the worries and cares of yesterday behind you, and do not be concerned for tomorrow. God has given you 24 hours to live at one time. All else "Let go and let God." Walk this day with your hand in Mine and together We will have the victory!

HEARD AND OBEYED

Every time I call a child of Mine to do the work I have for him I expect to be heard and to be obeyed. Now I don't call anyone until I know he is listening, eager, and waiting, this provides Me with confidence that once I call I will not be disappointed and I will not embarrass or put someone "on the spot" unnecessarily. Every work of Mine will be useless to Me and the one I call if conditions aren't proper. This is why some of My loved ones haven't been called yet, and this is why I can't just ask and have My way fulfilled. We are in this work for the Father together and until the children are ready the Holy Spirit, I [Jesus], and Our Father all stand by and wait. NOW Our waiting time is fast diminishing, and God will call time, and events will proceed leaving everyone in the place each has provided for himself.

"They that wait upon the Lord shall renew their strength." Wait in peace and expectation. Let the waiting be a drawing closer to the Lord, a seeking of His face. During this time experience His love. Let it engulf you and feed your soul. Let your mind be flooded with His peace, love, and joy. Your Father in heaven has all these blessings and more for you. Have a receptive soul, looking longingly to a loving God as your source. Listen for His soft voice of love showing the way and lifting you up. His plan for your life brings about the Spiritual growth necessary. Submit today unto the Lord and receive His direction, love and a new strength. Walk in victory hand in hand with your loving Heavenly Father.

A TRUE CALL

When will all My children come to Me with hearts open and willing to be filled with My truth, power, and ways? Only when they call on Me with a true call, a call of their heart to My heart, seeking only to know My way for them and not any other way. I eagerly am waiting for this heart change and you also must be single-minded about the things in your life right now. This time given will quickly come to an end, hear Me in this, soon the great longed for arrival in the clouds will come and I will gather the "ready virgins" to take them into their long dreamed of goal for His Family, to finally be all His, ready for the next growth into His arms. Come dear ones, no further delay is blessed!

When you received the Holy Spirit your spirit was renewed. You are your spirit, you have a soul and you live in a body. You soul has always joined with the flesh but now must be led by your renewed spirit and the Holy Spirit within. Our desire is the soul be renewed and saved. There is a daily battle waging between the soul and the body against the Spirit. The word tells Us "As many as are led by the Spirit of God, they are the Sons of God." Also, "Greater is He that is in you than he that is in the world." Be submissive to the Holy Spirit and let the Spirit be the leader in your life.

CREATOR'S WILL

It is with every breath My children take bringing Me closer to them that I find great pleasure, and I am blessed. Yes, dear ones as you live and breath I find tremendous joy in what the Father has planned and executed. All heaven and earth is coming to the "time of revelation," when the Father releases His hold on eternity and lets all the children come into His arms forever. The armies of Heaven are waiting to see this great event. Just before you now is the final act of family forming! Time must release its hold on God's children and then will come the moving of completion in the hearts and lives of His loved ones. Look up in heavenly anticipation for it is the Great Creator's will that is being formed then released.

Let My presence enfold you and bring forth the goodness I have for you. Submit to My presence and receive the blessings. God is love; let this love become a part of you. Be saturated in My mercy, peace, and love. Call out My name, acknowledge Me in all things. Let your words reflect your godly inner man and not the self or the world. Remember all power comes from Me, and all wisdom and peace. Always remember I am you source your loving Heavenly Father. You are My child, created for a purpose. I have a plan for your life. Will you walk with Me, will you submit to My will for you? Doing so will bring forth the victory filled with blessings forevermore!

GREAT VALUE

When all I've done for you suddenly becomes quite apparent you will have "spurt growth" of great value. Yes, I can snap you out of your lethargy and quickly turn your way toward Our goals. Growth in My loved ones has many facets, some are hidden growth of the heart, others are desire changes, there are heart turnings that open loves long locked doors, and then there is your head [mind] turning to things of the Spirit. Trust Me in all these areas by praying about your new walk with Me. Talk with Me about your hearts desire and I will share with you My heart's desire for Us. Every day is your opportunity to grow as you please, but why don't you ask Me to help you grow as I please!

Be steady on the course you are on. Persevere in peace, confident that I am with you. Keep your mind attuned to Me. "Let that mind be in you that is in Jesus Christ." When in doubt, wait on Me. Seek My face, listen for My voice, and experience My presence. "In His presence is fullness of joy." Let that joy permeate your soul and reflect to all others. There is joy in your walk with the Lord. Over-come the difficulties of the world and let His presence bring joy into your life. Expect victory!

MY WORK

Do not move in haste, but wait upon Me knowing that I am the source of all that you should be doing. My work is truly My work so seek to be obedient and doing only the things I lead you to do. No work is worthwhile unless there is only one place direction comes from, so watch carefully where you are going and why! Every day should become more purpose oriented, My purposes not yours. Truly there is a path that's right for you and your's. Truly there is a path that's right for you and you shall walk it, but it must be in trust knowing I am your guide and director. Never doubt the worth of purpose or the direction of movement because I will be the light of leading showing the way. Only My way from now on will be doing the will of the Father. One direction from One source forevermore!

Walk forward slowly, confidently, knowing that God is watching over you. There will be trials and tribulations along the way but you are to fear not for I am with you. Walk in a bubble of peace and love, which is in My presence. You are to overcome, to call on Me regularly and expect new strength, wisdom, and power. For I am your Heavenly Father and together all things are possible. "I can do all things through Christ who strengthens me." Trust Me, My children. Trust in the word I have given to you. Let it be constantly on your lips, My words of life and fullness, My promises to you. Remember Me in praise and worship. Praise opens the windows of heaven so that My blessings can be poured out.

BATTLE FOR LIFE

There are very few of My children who do just what I desire or ask, for they all are in a battle of life. This struggle, that I allow, proves itself by showing the results of what My loved ones accomplish. Many are doing the things I desire, many are led by Our Holy Spirit, and many are there who will receive rewards and blessings from the Father of all. Always keep these things in mind when you teach and talk to My loved ones. The fruit of the Spirit is displayed rarely in total or completeness, and that also is as I have planned. No worthwhile endeavor ever comes easily or without trials or tribulations, this I'm saying so you won't be discouraged by events surrounding you. Never look at the physical results to judge the worth of an endeavor. I am the rewarder and I see behind all happenings. I know the inside and the outside of all that occurs. Trust and obey, this is blind faith in action, which I reward handsomely!

Be in constant prayer, it is your connection with the Lord. The world and God's children are in need of your prayers. "The effectual fervent prayer of a righteous man availith much." Take My words to heart and talk to your Heavenly Father. When the Lord puts someone or some situation on your heart take it immediately to the Lord. Be led by the Holy Spirit in your prayer life. Remember, "You have not because you ask not." The Father is waiting for your prayers. He has ministering spirits [angels] waiting to minister to His children. Be a channel of love and blessings to others through your prayers. Pray without ceasing.

SCHOOL OF THE SPIRIT

The learning process I teach is the only way My children truly will know Me. Every child of Mine must report to the school of the Spirit and learn what My Holy Spirit has for each one. No one will be lifted up and given purpose from Me that I have not taught, led, and guided. All direction meaningful to life comes from My Spirit to each child. The learning process is not just the same, I have many ways to teach, but all who are led by My Spirit have listened in their heart and learned obedience to become successful. Never miss the teaching the Holy Spirit has for you.

In My care life is protected and is made whole and useful. "Let go and let God." Give yourself up to the will of God. Can you truly say the word, "Thy will be done, in me and through me, Oh Lord my strength and my redeemer," and let go of your will? The self is a strong influence, but "Greater is He that is in you than he that is in the world." You must choose the path you will take, self or the will of the Lord; submission is a part of "trust and obey." As you trust in your Heavenly Father submission will come as He has the best plan for you. His will will take you through the struggle and bring victory in the end. His way is filled with blessings.

POLICY OF LIVING

Just as I give you good words and kind greetings you should do also with all whom you meet. Make this a policy of living an acceptable life until We all meet in the air. All My children are family and I will release new blessings to those who follows this pattern before the time of completion. Remember always who you are and to whom you belong and represent. Show Our togetherness by your daily actions, that others may know Me and follow Me. I am seeking to come forth more through My dear ones, speak this to all who will listen and acknowledge they are Mine. This is a very simple, but very necessary lesson for these times. My love must be spread to counter the evil forces being released at this time. It is good to read and know, but better to obey and go!

Walk in the path I have prepared for you. Your strength will be renewed, your wisdom increased. Let your faith be the covering that sees you through. Your faith is the lifeline between you and Me and without faith there is no connection between Us. To increase your faith you must study the word and believe what I have said. Put My words and promises in your heart and on your lips. They are life to you. Let them become reality to you and not the things of the world and self. Call on Me constantly as a child seeks guidance from his father. I am your loving Heavenly Father. My way is the way of blessings.

DAWN COMES

When dawn comes My children see by its light, so it is and will be when it dawns upon My loved ones that I desire them to rise up like the sun each morning that I might shine the light of My wisdom upon their hearts. How can I teach if I have no students in My school of the Spirit? Yes this is a most necessary lesson for these times. And I will see that all hear it. Come dear ones and let Us enjoy this very last time of close visitation in the flesh for soon, very soon, We will all be One in the Spirit, and I will have My precious family closer to Me than ever before!

Rest in Me and turn all things over to Me. You are free in the soul as you repent your sins and seek My forgiveness. You are strong in the body as you receive My healing power. Your human spirit has been renewed by the power of the Holy Spirit. All of your being has been or can be renewed and made whole by your submission to Me. My children, My love is ever drawing you closer. Receive My forgiveness, My healing power, My wisdom, and walk with Me on the path I have prepared for you. Receive the love, peace and joy I have for you through your Holy Spirit. Begin now to enjoy the heavenly benefits saved up for you in heaven, and overcome the worldly obstacles. Go through and learn the lessons needed in every situation with My help and direction. Victory is near; persevere for I am with you!

FULL CONTROL

When I call a child of Mine into a ministry I am implying by that action that he must allow Me full control, not just times of ministry but of his whole life. There is no such thing as "part time" work with Me. A commitment made with Me is a forever thing with Me and it must be so with whosoever I call. I will pour out My love and blessings in My guidance and control expecting those loving actions to be released and extended through My chosen ones to My needy ones. There is a flow of love that begins in My heart, overflows to and through My children until all of My saved ones become One. This is My plan for all My children, no one is separate, no one is special, and no one is better than anyone else. All are Mine and all are One in Me. My love extends to and through all My family with never-ending flow.

Let your mouth show forth the righteousness of God. The word tells you "The mouth of a righteous man is a well of life." Are you speaking life or death? Are the words you speak acceptable to your Heavenly Father? Will you pray the scripture "May the words of my mouth and the meditations of my heart be acceptable in thy sight, Oh Lord my strength and my redeemer." What is buried in your heart will come out of your mouth. Discipline in this area is important. Let your words be of love, of caring, in peace and in patience, always lifting up. Praise God and bless others by the words of your mouth.

SOURCE OF WISDOM

The forming of a class of students will only be worthwhile when I am the gatherer. Just as I direct nations so do I lead and guide small groups. In My world I am to be the source of all wisdom and activity of worth. When My loved ones call on Me for *growth principals* then will they find a true path of intelligent progress. From each student to entire generations proper growth will occur when I am called to lead and be the source of all service. This note is a reminder that you who are Mine must always keep My purposes and goals foremost in all of your pursuits. A teaching that says, " man's ways of promoting victory will always win," is self-destruction in the making, only My ways will prevail.

WONDER WALK

The working of life in a man should be left up to Me, but I will never take you over or interfere with your free will. My dear children all that you are or ever will be is in My hands and the sooner you release all of your "self" to Me the sooner I can draw you into My place for you. When this occurs then I have release to bring you daily into a wonder walk of beginning eternity. Come dear ones and seek to find that release in you that I so desire. The giving up of self is the last and most important work you have and the most important work for completeness. Seek more of My word, more of My desires, more of My ways for you. Come draw closer every day and soon, so soon We will be together in foreverness.

My children put all things in My hands. Rest in Me and you will be renewed. Clear your mind of earthly cares and call on Me and you will be given wisdom. Repent your sins and receive My forgiveness and you will have peace. Let My love flow through you to all others and you will have joy. Life with Me is truly one of love, peace and joy as you learn the Spiritual lessons necessary. Let My will be done in you and through you and My blessings will surround you always. Let go and let God and all things will be done in decency and order. God's love is your blanket of protection, your strength, your peace, and it will guide your way.

LESSON OF LOVE

There are many ways My children learn the things I bring to them, but the lesson of My love is the most successful. My love is always new, My love is always on time and directed properly. There are no substitutes for My love because there is only one love source. Man's love is never ongoing, never fulfilling and never endless. Man seeking man's love will only find faults and disappointments unless that love flows from My love stream. Yes man's love can be My love flowing. I desire man to be My love vendor, but not selling, just releasing freely the love I give. Come dear ones and learn about this love flowing from Me. In the stillness when We meet I will give this love in lessons worth learning, come to My school of the Spirit and listen, hear, and see, then be My love source flowing forever!

Time spent with Me brings peace and a quiet Spirit. It develops patience and brings forth knowledge. Let My will for you be known in Our quiet time together. Let My healing power flow through your being and renew your strength. I am your source of all things and it is My desire to release all these blessings to you. I am with you as you go through the trials and tribulations necessary for your Spiritual growth. Persevere through these times having faith that you will have the victory as We stand together. See and acknowledge that your faith is growing, as you trust in Me. Remember the many answered prayers and the joy of the Lord you have experienced. Remember I am your source. Call on Me constantly and walk the way I have planned for you.

THE TIME IS NOW FOR THE FINISHING TOUCH

It will be Our pleasure and joy to teach the children the lessons of the Spirit. Your Holy Spirit has so much wisdom and guidance to bring to all the Bride of Christ and the time is NOW to begin. Yes, the lessons in the school of the Spirit are the finishing touch upon the children of God bringing great pleasure and joy to both the Father of all and all whom He Father's. Preparation for the journey ahead will release great wisdom and guidance, blessings, and joy to God's loved ones, and great pleasure and rewards to the Glory of the Trinity of Love. Come dear ones open your heart willingly to God's silent school of the Spirit and you will find your chosen walk with Jesus.

Anticipate the blessings of each day. Rise early and expect and receive God's love and peace in your heart. Trust your loving Heavenly Father to supply all your needs according to His riches in Glory through Jesus Christ, "Let your faith build as you claim, "I can do all things through Christ who strengthens me." Use God's word; claim it as your own. It is truly His promise to you. Walk this day in love and all things will be added to you. Walk this day with Me and let My love fill your soul and you will be the salt of the earth I have intended you to be.

WHEN

When is a time question My children are always asking, I also look foreword to the "When Time" of each child of Mine because there are many when's. When will I die you ask? I say when you truly live! When will I be raptured My children wonder, I say when will you truly be Mine? When will I find happiness they say, I answer when will you truly be Mine? When will I find out what I should do? I say when will you learn to ask Me and then listen? When are We to be One they say, I SAY HOW LONG MUST I WAIT FOR YOU TO OBEY? My dear ones all of the when answers lie in the Father's heart and your only task is to seek Me more, listen more, and then obey more. Soon We will be living in the everlasting time of "when", where the Father never stops happenings.

Keep your thoughts focused on Me and your thoughts will be God inspired. Trust the "ideas" you have are from Me. Maintain a connecting channel between Us in praise, in prayer, in worship, and in the word. In this manner I can pour out My blessings upon you and give you directions and answers you require. Build your faith by truly accepting the peace and wisdom I give you, knowing it is from your heavenly Father. Be a quiet Spirit confident that I am leading you and supplying all your needs. Relax in My love and peace. Anticipate the joy of the Lord and the blessings that follow. Love others as you love Me. I am your source of love so it is always available. Overcome the world and walk in My love!

PUSH FOR MORE

It is in consistent seeking more of Me and from Me that true Spiritual growth occurs. I encourage all My loved ones to be pushing for more from Me, always striving, always asking, always receiving, and it will be in this manner that I can reward and bless each one. Your course with Me is not one waiting without purpose, but instead is waiting with great expectations and high hopes of many blessings coming forth. The goal to seek is My purpose for you, not your desire for your own blessing. I can give greater rewards than you can conceive; I just need you to believe that is true and then follow as I lead. Test and see what a team We can be!

Still the mind let My peace fill your soul and body. In this way you can receive what I have for you. Cast your cares on Me so you may be free to receive. Today operate in love and righteousness. Go slow and let My peace prepare the way. See all in love as through the eyes of Jesus. Be sensitive, be compassionate, and your thoughts will be My thoughts. Today, "Let that mind be in you which was also in Christ Jesus." Doing so will fill you with My joy!

MIND PICTURES

In My teaching I bring many words into play, but no word is more important than another. It takes many teachings, many experiences and much effort to bring knowledge, wisdom, and understanding to My children. Always take proper time when presenting a subject I bring to you. Do not hurry, speak fast, or push from one idea to another. Good teaching is like a stain that's hard to remove, because it took a while to soak in. Time is important so use it wisely, but more important is the purpose of a lesson. Give mind pictures clarifying the explanation, these help instill the idea being told. Clear thinking will release clear pictures of worth aiding the understanding of the story told. Use a loving approach in all your openings.

Enjoy your life and be thankful for it. You have been placed in a particular family in a special area and circumstance for your Spiritual growth. You also will effect the lives of those around you. Consider all things as planned by God for your growth or help for others. Be the salt of the earth and the light of the world with God's love shinning out of you. Make each happening and each contact positive. Lift the spirits of all you meet. Bring the light into this world of darkness. Let joy overflow in your life. Bring this joy and laughter to others that their spirits may be lifted, truly a happy heart and laughter is medicine to the soul. Lift those around you with encouraging words of life and love. This will increase the joy of the Lord in your life.

A PROPER HEART

I give many lessons to My children because no one way will suffice. To properly teach such diverse groups takes many approaches and much patience. Lesson giving is to flow on and on because I am forever and I have so much to release. Teachers are in a special place with Me because teaching is close to My heart. To be a good teacher requires a proper heart. A heart for truth is a prime requirement, so truth seekers become My chosen source of worthwhile instructors. Always look carefully into material sources because the beginning point must be pure for uncontaminated information. Seek truth only in the places I lead you to, and learn lessons I bring you; this way your guidance will be proper. Keep lessons clear and simple. Complex stories may be intriguing but attention is lost in many wanderings.

"Greater is He that is in you than he that is in the world." I, the Holy Spirit, am God within you, and I am all of God and His power. I have for you the overcoming power and wisdom to handle any situation. But you must call on Me, acknowledge Me, and listen for My voice. I have been sent to you to be your helper and your comforter. You have free will to call upon Me or to go your own way. You choose My help or reject it. Which will it be? I have blessings of love, peace, and joy for you, long-suffering, gentleness, and goodness, even faith, meekness and self-control; all these are available to you because you are a child of God. Receive all God has for you and truly let Me be your Heavenly helper.

OBEDIENCE

The leading of My children has now become a true necessity because of the short time left. It is a most important task that I set before you, that is tell all who will listen I'm coming soon, very very soon! Each one must wake up to this call because I can still do great things to draw them quickly into a closer walk. Obedience to My call, and this obedience must be to what I say to them personally, will prove of great value and bring their lives into a closer walk. A closer walk now will bring great rewards and blessings for their eternal position and place with Me. Carefully consider what has just been said, place it foremost in your plans and heart!

God's word is powerful, and it is creative. Almighty God created this earth and the universe by speaking the word. As His children, joint-heirs with Jesus, use His word as a force for healing, for blessings, and for praise and worship. Use His word audibly that that your soul may be convinced of its truth. Claim it in the name of Jesus. "God's word is medicine to all your flesh." It is love made real in your life. Claim the promises God made to you in His word. They are for you. Increase your faith by the words of your mouth. "Faith cometh by hearing and hearing by the word of God." Truly let the words of your mouth be acceptable to your loving Heavenly Father.

A CONTINUOUS OUT- FLOWING

When will all that I teach be all that My children do? Only when they all are truly Mine in their head, heart, and ways. Never will I give up or leave any one of them. I will pursue until all is truly lost or truly gained. The lost are only lost because of their doing, My doing is forever salvation, but also My doing is only where reception is desired. There must be open arms and open hearts for Me to draw with My Father's love. His love is forever and I too am a recipient of that continuous out flowing. The Father is truly Heaven's source of ever flowing love and I too am its release. My dear children this is what We are calling you into, the ever flowing of God's love. Our desire is that you choose Us, choose life and know loves ever flowing Source. To see things with the eyes of faith is to cause it to manifest in the material!

The power of life or death is in the tongue. Which will you choose? Let your words be My words, words of love, of light, of peace and joy. Keep your mind filled with the things of the Lord. See others as Jesus sees them. Cast out all critical and negative thinking and replace it quickly with the word of God. Let your words reflect a mind filled with the love of God, His grace, peace, and patience. Your Heavenly Father will be your covering and your lead. Think on Him!

TOOL OF WISDOM

When I bring a word of love, wisdom, or direction I expect it to be welcomed, read, considered and used to help others, and the one with whom I share it. Just to talk for talks sake will scatter and waste the good tool of wisdom passed on. Think about the better use of the "word to the wise" that I'm bringing daily to you. Think how you can better use what is said or read in private, maybe you can truly help others by spreading what you hear or read from or about Me. If you make an effort to apply the truth given, then I will made an effort to bring more and more to your doorstep. Come be a dispenser and displayer of My truth, wisdom, and ways. The outflowing of worth from Me should be continued as the outflowing of love from you.

Rise up and know that a loving God has chosen you. He created all things and He is your Heavenly Father. His love surrounds you and floods your soul if you are an open vessel. Receive God's love and peace and be a channel of blessings to others. Learn to have joy regardless of the situation. In every circumstance learn the lesson that is presented. Go through whatever comes your way confident that God is helping you to overcome. The blessings offered by the Holy Spirit are released when you call on them. Acknowledge the great gifts of the fruit of the Spirit. They are yours when you release them into your life. Among these gifts are faith, patience, and self-control. Put these in effect in your life today and victory will be yours!

SOON COMING

Never will all be right on this earth until the New Heavens and New Earth are released, then only My loved ones will be present to enjoy it. Until then this is a place of work, growth and learning with trials, and tribulations. The good that comes now will be from the good God releases. This could be an oh so short time if everyone were given over to Jesus early in life, and then they would just flow in His love released, but that was not the Father's plan. Free will given must be just that, so man has his choice. My dear ones who have found Jesus seek out the lost ones now and tell them how much Jesus sacrificed for them, how much He loves them, and how soon He is coming again. This is a simple message, why is it so difficult for you to give it out? Just put self down and lift Jesus up, it can be so rewarding.

Let the fullness of God and His love be upon you. Receive the wonderful blessings your Father has for you. Be led by the Holy Spirit within and God's promises to you can become a reality in your life. Be an open channel, free to receive God's blessings and to allow them to flow out to all others. "Thy will be done in me and through me, oh Lord my strength and my redeemer." Let this word be the guide and direction of your life.

MY KINGDOM

The continual seeking for a closer walk with Me will bring surprising results. It is in this striving that I can judge your desire and then your worth to the Kingdom. More should be spoken about My Kingdom. I don't hear much Kingdom talk anymore so why don't you start thinking Kingdom ways and asking Me more about your place in the kingdom? Yes I will have a wonderful Kingdom and you will be setting a foundation for a high place in My Kingdom. I give out great rewards and blessings to My children where I find ones who listen, and hearing rightly, and then they obey. All growth in My Kingdom comes from this type of attention being given daily not just hit or miss. Take from this note today all that it implies and give Me something to work with in your life.

Trust and obey the Lord and your life will have meaning. To obey is to be obedient; to be obedient is to be submissive. To be submissive is to humble self and do the will of the Father. Have a quiet loving Spirit toward all authority. Let not rebellion reign in your heart. A rebel against authority is a rebel against God. "Submit yourselves therefore to God. Resist the devil and he will flee from you." Thus submission to God becomes power, power to resist the devil. Let the joy of the Lord fill your soul as you seek to become a submissive One.

DIFFERENT STYLES

In the continuing effort of teaching, I find it necessary to repeat lessons in order to make effective the words sent forth previously. To enclose thoughts in new phrases and different styles brings out the driving force of words previously spoken. Many new thoughts are only old ideas looked at differently. If you become aware of old things being said in a new manner maybe you should pay more attention to it because it has been shown to be most important by its new presentation. Only to those thinking alert ones are deep things of hidden worth brought to the surface of daily attention. Attention and clear thinking applies to all I bring to My children, but especially to the ones who will pass truth on in a believable, understanding method. Seek, My dear ones, to be one who passes on truth understandable!

God is an awesome God, He reigns over heaven and earth and yet He calls you His children. He loves each one with a special and individual love. He has a plan for each member of His family. He will bring before you the lessons needed for Spiritual growth, so you can have a closer walk with Him. God's desire is His children should call on Him, rest in Him, and have faith in all His promises and especially to love Him and love one another. God is love and His desire is His love becomes a part of you, that your life will be directed and ruled by the love of God. Walk in this love and live in His presence!

CHECK IT OUT

The growing concern I have is why aren't you drawing closer all of the time? Come dear ones start by believing I am in you and then thanking Me for helping in every situation. Walk as if all this is true, and I will be released to make it so. Your believer needs activation, your wanter must disappear and My wanter must be the only one on the scene. Come think about what has just been said! It is so easy, come into My Spirit realm and then move in the flesh world as if you see things from My viewpoint. What an exciting time We will have If you try; I'll be there, check it out and see.

Persevere for the time is short. I am always with you and My strength is your strength, My power is available to you. Rest in Me and receive all you need. "They that wait upon the Lord shall renew their strength, they shall rise up on wings of eagles." Rise up now confident that I will supply all your needs according to My riches in Glory through Jesus Christ.

PUSH OF TROUBLE

The continuing trouble I give ALL My children is the only way to prod them into the place of love I have prepared. When My love doesn't draw them the push of trouble seems to stir up enough response that I have something to work with. Whatever it takes, for the Father of All is eagerly waiting the catching away just ahead. Nothing can stop this great culmination of God's love gathering. The Father's heart cries out for this wonderful moment so longed for and anticipated. Never again and never before has anything like this happened. My dear ones can't you catch the breath of God breathing His love upon you, calling in your heart "Come My dear ones quickly finish up your walk and fully be Mine." Your answer lies in your response, what will it be? Do not diminish or slack off in these times for they are your last chance to get up and run into His arms forever!

Be alert, watch carefully what is going on around you. Be thankful for the blessings bestowed upon you, for God's beautiful creation. Pray often for the situations and people I put on your heart. Be led by the Holy Spirit. Walk each day with a quiet spirit in My peace, so the directions of the Holy Spirit will be made known to you. When necessary rest, rest in Me, that you may take on My strength and learn of My will for you. Remember, "My yoke is easy and My burden is light." My Glory will bring joy to your soul.

AWARENESS TIME

It is in the "Awareness times" that your Spiritual growth moves faster. This means you should learn to be positive of Our presence, directing, and moving you. As you comply We are released to help you more in this endeavor. "Always believe" your growth is closely tied to this procedure. Now more than ever the Father is pushing for His children to be walking in the paths of Our given direction. This is a necessary requirement for the "Catching Away" to occur. Preparation is the order of the day for all Our seeking, listening ones. The teaching of this preparation must start to be talked about more. My Son's Bride has much still to do to be what and where I seek them to be. Attention to growing in this manner is a most necessary step into the "Completion Time" set by the Father. Call out now, when time is given to you, for more teaching along this line of endeavor.

"This is the day the Lord has made. I will rejoice and be glad in it." Let this be your theme for today. Oh My children enjoy the life you have been given, whether it is in rest, in work unto the Lord or in ministering to others. All days have been created for your good. Spiritual growth comes afterwards when you do not realize it. In My rest and waiting upon Me comes My peace. Putting My word into your hearts brings about health and wisdom. In prayer, praise and worship We are brought closer together. "In all your ways acknowledge Him and He will direct your paths." Walk this day acknowledging My presence with you and you shall be victorious.

BEFORE YOU

Keep the things of the Lord before you more. See each hour as a new walk in the way prepared for you. Do not just wander on your own without proper goals and direction. It is the times that are driving the way you should go. Listen more carefully to what I have to say to you personally, and then direction will become apparent and purpose will be given the driving force to carry you to victory. Never doubt that you are a victor on your walk with Me, because doubting will disintegrate drive's purpose and failure will be given a path to flow in. All time is made for My purpose to flower, so don't block My purpose any longer. Our driving force is the Father's time and purpose accomplished. Keep this in mind more, because you have a challenge each day to be what the Father of all has called for you to be. Listen, hear, and obey, this is the most important time in your life right now!

Go slow, walk in peace, and walk in My presence and in My love. Let your attitude be one of love, goodwill and joy. Allow My love to pour through you and be a beacon of light to those around you. See others through My eyes, always accepting not critisizing, and do this with compassion. In the little things have patience and peace, nothing disturbing your peace of mind. In this flow of peace My will will be done. Remember, "All is well" because I am with you. With Me you are an over-comer. "Greater is He that is in you than he that is in the world."

A USEFUL TOOL

When a man truly awakens to the Spirit realm I'm drawing him to, then and only then, can I make him a useful tool for My kingdom. Yes, My Kingdom is only made up of true children led all of the time by My Holy Spirit. Why are My so-called churches so intent on missing My truth, only because self has such tight control on most of them. True progress in My kingdom is only found by following My desires all of the time. Time is given to the children as a gift to be opened to find Me, not anybody or anything else! Seek inside of you for all the things you desire to be about you. I am the only source to be sought, and there is no end to what you may find, but searching is started from inside of you after you are born again. Only by being "Spirit Led" can I bring My kingdom children home. It is the seeking more from My Holy Spirit that I can give increase in My Kingdom.

Imagine in your heart the glories to come. Think about the over-whelming presence of God with His love and power flooding your life, and realize the up-coming joy everlasting that will be yours. Contemplate the compassion of the Lord coming upon you and going forth to all others. These blessings can be yours now, in your earthly body, to the degree that you submit to My will and walk with Me. Walk in accordance with My word. Let your faith grow and trust in the promises I have given you. In prayer, praise, and worship keep the connection We have strong. Be that channel of blessings. Trust your Heavenly Father for all things, for I am trustworthy and always with you.

BURSTING FORTH

The continuous drawing closer to Me will bring you to your "bursting forth" place. Just keep on the seeking path and Glory will be your surrounding. Every flower that desires air and sunshine grows out of earth's cool darkness. Substance comes from the dark places within and few people give much attention to that fact. From deep inside of My children I am stirring and awakening the Spirit to bring forth Spiritual things from My Kingdom larder. Just let truth be the sustainer of your Spirit then your soul will have to pay attention. All victory comes from Me so let Me have all of your self so the new Spirit within can fly with Me. Yes We can soar through time and find great treasures to tap.

My children remember you have an advocate sitting on the right hand of God interceding on your behalf. His name is Jesus, your Lord and Savior, your redeemer. Let this fact strengthen your faith. My word tells you to ask anything in Jesus' name and believe and you shall receive it. Believe My word to you, trust your heavenly advocate Jesus and trust your Heavenly Father who has an everlasting love for you. Let your faith increase as you meditate on these facts.

TROUBLING TIMES

When I bring light and knowledge to My children I expect them to reflect, show faith, and be an exhibit of such blessings. Through their obedience I then expect to see other children blessed, encouraged, helped, and loved. My true disciples are the willing workers, led by My Holy Spirit, showing the lost My love for them. This is to be a way of life for My true ones. Why are so few walking in this path of victory, as I desire? No one can follow two masters and be loyal to one only, but My children are constantly doing just that. They follow "self," and then give Me some time, and if they are further along they follow Me then self sometimes. Total obedience to Me is the only path for truth seekers to walk. This must be taught more because of the troubling times ahead.

What do you need today? Strength? "I can do all things through Christ who strengthens me," Do you need peace? "My peace I give you, not as the world gives, give I to you." Joy? "In thy presence is fullness of joy."

Do you need wisdom? "Let that mind be in you which was also in Jesus Christ." The answers to your needs are all found in My word. My promises to you, that I am faithful to perform, are yours when We are walking together. Lean on Me for I am your Heavenly Father. I have a great love for you, My Creation, My child. In these days of much activity, step out confidently, knowing I am with you, supplying all of your needs. Be led by the indwelling Holy Spirit, My gift to you, to be your comforter and your helper. My will for you will bring much joy. Let go and let Us walk together forever.

ALWAYS FOREVER

The training of My loved ones is an endless task of love. Love because the Father has decreed His love shall go and flow forever through the channel of His children. All works, all desires, all activities must stem from and be sourced from the Father's great love. No child of God is separated from love. Love is all, love is substance and vapor, love is never still, never stagnates, love blossoms anew daily. Seek love and it is always found, desire love and it is never withheld, pursue love and it is always caught, send love and it never ceases. Be love's source and you are of God, with God and God's child. Demand, ask for, seek and search for love, it will always be yours. Be love and you are always forever eternal.

My child remember you are a temple, a temple of the Holy Spirit. Within you lies the power of God, the peace of God, and the love of God. Also available in you is joy, gentleness, goodness, faith, meekness, self-control, long suffering and patience. All these attributes of God, these great blessings, can be and should be yours. By submitting self to the will of God you can receive what God has for you. Acknowledge the Holy Spirit within; be led by the Holy Spirit to become children of God. Win your victory with the leading of God's gift to you, the Holy Spirit.

LISTEN

This is a day that I give, as is each day, but make today My day and I will bring many new blessings to you. Make each day My day and your walk will be strewn with rewards and blessings for My entire children roundabout. To test what is said will take your dedication to following, seeking and believing; therefore each day can be special as you believe and achieve in willing obedience to the life I unfold before you. Keep this on your heart and mind, "Listen to My Spirit within you to know the why, what, and where of each days." I am not a mystery to those who are obedient to My word, written and\or spoken, so know this truth and be drawn into the blessings of hearing, knowing, and obeying.

Let the joy of the Lord spring forth from your soul. Rest in Me to receive the peace that will release this joy. "Laughter is medicine to the body." See always the happy side of life, there is darkness and there is light. Walk in the light for it is of your Heavenly Father. In the light of the Lord is joy forevermore. "The joy of the Lord is my strength." God desires that you receive what He has for you, "In thy presence is fullness of joy, at thy right hand there are pleasures for evermore.

DO NOT DO!

In My working time with each child of Mine I find many ways to encourage and guide, but I don't find so many listening or obeying if they are listening. I must find good listeners, but when I do I have to search out the ones who are doers! Why is that? To hear a plan or direction given doesn't mean any more than just to read something without being motivated to do. "TO DO," now there is the stumbling block stopping most of My listeners. You should be aware that the more you read, the more you hear, the more you are shown, builds up a sorry case against you when you DO NOT DO!

Oh My child, rest in Me and receive what God has for you. Let the peace that passeth understanding dwell in your heart. This will release the blessings I have stored up for you. In peace your prayers are more effective. Praise and worship the Lord until you feel that peace flooding your being. Your prayer life is so important. Pray knowing I hear you supplications. Pray in faith and believe My promises to answer prayers said in My name. There is power in the name of Jesus. Walk in My presence and be led by the Holy Spirit and My Glory will cover you all the days of your life.

OUR JOY

The molding and making of a willing, working child of Mine is My great pleasure. It is a blessing and Our joy when obedience flowers into fruitful work displaying My hand of blessings to the lost and needy. Response is welcomed when We reach out with purpose and We find a ready, eager worker of Our Love. Seek to be Our blessing to the lost and needy ones and you will find your life fulfilled and your larder full. Only listening doers will find all that I have prepared for them. So many lose their rewards and blessings I release when willing work is given and not done as We desire. All growth comes quickly to Our children who listen, and hearing rightly engage fully in Our endeavors.

You are free to walk uprightly and boldly as your sins have been forgiven. You have been cleansed by the power of the blood of Jesus. God truly sees you through Jesus. You have been made righteous through the sacrifice of Jesus. Therefore go forth in love and compassion for others, walk the path God has prepared for you. You are under the grace of God, so walk as the child of God you were created to be. Be humble and childlike that you may be teachable. Listen for directions from the Holy Spirit and walk according to My word, and My commandments. Live constantly in peace and joy, trusting your Heavenly Father to show the way. He is always with you; acknowledge Him by your love.

LISTEN AND DO

When I bring a word to you that persists, and keeps itself before you, will you ignore it? Would My speaking aloud in your ears make you pay attention to the things I desire to say to you? Are you willing to listen and then will you decide to obey? What method will truly wake you up and cause you to hear, listen, and desire to become doers of the things I say? My dear ones tell Me and I will do the thing or things you say that will cause you to believe, obey, and achieve the rewards and blessings I have already prepared to give to you. I died for you, suffered for you, acted out in the flesh the path you should walk, what more can I do than write to you like this? Come read My Bible, listen to My Spirit talk, be My doers and then We will be One!

Jesus is in the midst of you, beckoning for you to follow. He wants you close to Him so He can protect you and fill you with His love. Can you walk with Him? Can you say and mean "Thy will be done in me and through me, Oh Lord my strength and redeemer." His desire is that you come humbly as a little child into His arms and loving care. He would that you follow His way, as it is the only way to the throne of God. You have been given free will. Can you freely choose Jesus and not the world or self? The blessings are abundant and He is always there to lift you up, and to carry you when you falter. Trust His promises and have the victory through your redeemer, Jesus Christ.

SAFE FOREVER

It will be by My power only that I build My Kingdom. My children must wholly, totally, submit their will to Me, that is the only way power in My children can bring them properly placed into My Kingdom, the only way they will be correctly motivated. Spiritual power can only be controlled by Me wherever I send it, allow it, or use it. My children can never control My Holy Spirit Power, I am the only God and there is none other. My children will always have My power available to them because We are, and will be forever, One. Our Oneness is Our life together, and together the Father has given Us everything! This control from The Father is a safeguard for Us forever.

The Glory of the Lord is all about you. In your mind's eye see His Glory and not the darkness in the world. For where sin is, God's righteousness does more abound. The greater power is God's light. The light always abolishes the darkness. Walk in the light, see the good all about you, and dwell in the Glory of God. Truly let the joy of the Lord be your strength. Know He is always with you, lifting you up. Be aware of His great love enfolding you and protecting you from evil. God is love. His love is forever!

ALL GOD

No action is more worthy than the action produced from love. Let My love in you be the instigator of your love's release toward others. Love is a subject unreachable in all of its ramifications, because I release to no one love's totality. To seek love, My love, is always successful, but to reach all love is a goal never obtained by My children for "all love" is "ALL GOD"! No path or desire is more worthy, no search more rewarding than the pursuit of love's release in a child of Mine. My love is never withheld when truth seeking love for love's purpose is pursued. To keep this goal is to stay close to Me, in close touch, and always obedient. It takes an open heart and willing ways to completely release self, but there is no other path for love's capture. True love is only found when truth is searched out in your heart, and then cleansing can take place. This is each child's true goal to pursue.

Another day, another blank page to be written upon your lives, your thoughts, and on your actions. Will this be a positive or a negative day? It is your choice. Your free will is in charge. I say choose goodness, not evil, kindness not cruelty, love not indifference. If your mind is stayed on Me these things are possible. Let My peace and joy fill you soul. Feel and walk in My love as I am always with you. Let understanding and compassion be your goal today. Others in this dark world need the light of Jesus; can you be that source of light, My child? Let it be obvious that you are a child of God that your Heavenly Father may be Glorified!

MORE AND MORE

When I set a man to follow My plan I will only allow him to wander a little. Once My plan is started I will pursue its completion vigorously. You should know this about Me, and then walk carefully in My plan for you. Your time has ceased when you embark on My plan, so stop reverting to your old ways and seeking to walk in the old paths familiar to you. We are together taking a new course; a different way and looking back will break the spell of righteousness building slowly to your eternal benefit. Know this, My plan is only My desire to bring great worth and blessings into your life with Me and as you grow in this knowledge you will lose old desires; they will be lost in the wonder of new wealth building to your benefit. Walk worthy and see all I say unfold around you more and more!

You are able through the power of Almighty God to do all things I have planned for you. Seek My face; desire to know My will for your life. Listen to My still quiet voice. Walk in complete faith that God is leading you and giving to you the necessary wisdom and strength to carry out His will. Do not be in a hurry, patience is a virtue. With a quiet Spirit be led by the Holy Spirit, having a willing and submissive Spirit and soul. Learn the lessons of each day, sometimes taking baby steps in your growth. All is important, and have a loving open attitude toward all things, especially My children. A caring, considerate loving attitude will open up the way. Go gently in love.

SOME MORE

Never look about you and miss My works or Me. I am always watching over you and caring for My children, most of them give Me no attention, or slight Me, but I watch over them anyway. It is the ones who know Me that should be aware of My presence, giving attention and care to what I am doing in their midst. How much have you missed? Do you know? I'm bringing this note to open your eyes, and make you aware of things on earth in the Spirit realm that you should awaken to. This is to enhance your Spiritual growth, and to make you notice My works more and more.

My children you are in My care so lean on Me more. Wait on Me for My timing is perfect, and have peace of mind for all is well. My plan is going forward. You are to learn the lessons daily that come your way, so have patience, peace, and goodwill to others. Let the joy of the Lord fill your heart, it will help you to understand My will for you. Have a merry heart for it is good medicine. As you read the word know it is for you. Take all the promises personally, because We are walking together and there are great blessings ahead of you.

THEIR ALL

When will My will be the will of all of My children? Only when they have prepared their hearts for Me in an acceptable manner. They are Mine but they haven't submitted their all. I can only bless with My blessings and rewards when steps are taken proving My children have given up self and received all from Me that I offer. I offer daily to My willing ones but they still need further cleansing and deliverance from theirs flesh self. All My children are Mine now but all My children have not yet risen to their appointed place. My patience is being stretched and My time is running out, how will I deal with this foot-dragging?

Your health is in My hands. Jesus said, "I have come that you may have life and that more abundantly." Trust in these words. Live the abundant life I have for you. Come to Me when difficulties arise, ask and you shall receive. I would that My children be strong and walk upright in My power and strength. Live daily in health. Do everything in peace. Draw closer to Me that your faith may grow. The burden I have for you is light, My yoke is easy. Come joyfully into any task I have brought before you, just know that I am in the midst of it, showing the way and giving strength. Walk with Me, dear child. My way is easy and a joy unto your heart.

CAN'T YOU TELL?

There are very few children of Mine that give Me their whole attention. Why would that be? Just because the world is so imposing! The body cries for attention, feeding, clothing, housing, and entertainment; the mind desires pleasures of all kinds when the other many things are taken care of. Yes the world about is a real attention getter, but can't that also be said of Me? I made the world and all that's in it, I created the heavens and the earth that man should know Me, am I so far away and unknowable that I should be ignored? Come My dear ones who have found Me, can't you tell the lost children what you've discovered? Isn't there anything you can be a witness of for Me? What is there that you know about Me that you can tell? Anything? Wake up dear ones, your time is very, very short to catch up where you should be!

Where there is life there is hope, and where is life there is God. God is the essence of all things. It is His power that holds all things together. In His love you were created and are loved. The Creator of the Universe is your Heavenly Father, your Abba Father! His love surrounds you and carries you through every situation. In your free will you may choose to walk away from Him, but He will never leave you. Knowing this, you should walk boldly in the way, learning the lessons of the way. This will bring about the Spiritual growth needed and God can shower you with His blessings. Live life abundantly!

THE GIFT

It is in the little things, given proper attention, that I build My kingdom. Always keep in touch with the insignificant, unseemly, and distraught for even through and by them I will bring new understanding and insight in My kingdom building. My world for you is built of good and bad only for the purpose of your proper schooling. How could you love white if black was never shown? All is presented for your education, but all is not given for your purpose or use, just for your proper choosing. How will I find true children if none of them ever run the race? How will you know Me if you never search? Is a jewel less worthy because it is so easy to find or because it is difficult to capture? Whether My children recognize the race they are in or not, whether they understand and give it all of their heart or not is left up to them. This is The Gift, whether it is eagerly pursued or just left lying untouched; it is theirs to choose!

Today do the will of God because yesterday is past and tomorrow has not yet come. Today is the NOW and you are to live in the NOW! This day, 24 hours, walk with Me, talk with Me, and listen to the voice of the Holy Spirit. Pray constantly that you stay close to Me. Praise and worship should be on your tongue for this will release the power and joy I have for you. I am with you so all things are possible. I have dispatched angels to watch over you. Now walk confidently in this knowledge, secure that as a child of God all things are possible through Jesus Christ. Your needs are being provided, and you are walking in My love and power. So truly, "You can do all things through Christ who strengthens you." Walk free in the victory!

SEEKING ONES

The true meaning of My Word is not buried and is not a secret to any of My seeking children. It is My delight to enlarge their knowledge and enhance their lives by their proper use and reception of My Word. My dear children use My Word in My Bible and I will make it alive in your hearts, heads, and body. Is not your body My residence? My temple? What kind of a place are you making for Me? Come dear ones awaken to the truth abounding throughout My Bible, aren't you anxious to see what I'll do next? I'm alive and well, but most of My church is only half alive.

My Spirit longs to see His gifts flowing, blessing the children and saving the lost ones. Where are you now on your walk with Me? Are We enjoying fruitful days with Spiritual gifts flowing? Why not?

The Lord is watching over all His children, His love is never ending. In the difficult days there may be lessons you are to learn. Go through each situation in patience and peace, confident that God's plan for you is a good and perfect one. Learn to lean on Him, to wait upon the Lord and your strength will be renewed. See each circumstance as a learning opportunity. Let God's love cover all for this too shall pass. Let all things draw you closer to your loving Heavenly Father; His love will carry you through.

OUR FOREVER

The working of My plans for man has always been an ongoing, ceaseless task of love. My work with and for My children is My source of never-ending pleasure. When My children are called home to "Our Forever" that will be the future that is dreamed of now by men, but man's dreams and hopes are so far from the true reality of what the Father has planned. Be assured that not one minute given to Me now will be a wasted effort, God's rewards are priceless and His love never stops. How can I convey such things to further inspire and capture your full attention? Listen My dear ones; "This time now present has more potential for your everlasting good than anytime of the past." The gathering time releases God's heart, to give more and more, to encourage, and to save more and more of His children. Make this time just before you the most concentrated effort of your lives, it will prove to be your most worthwhile time of effort ever spent doing God's work!

God's love abides and His love is the power, the force that rules the world. His love is also an individual force in the life of each of His children. He knows the lessons needed, He knows the sensitive and weak areas in your life. He has the solution to your problems. As your faith increases and you learn to lean on Him you will be an over-comer and grow Spiritually in your walk with Him. Look outward to others, to the beauty of the world about you. Be in an attitude of thanksgiving and praise for the blessings in your life. Let your mouth be filled with words of love and joy. Remember My word to you, "Whatsoever things are true, honest, just and pure; whatsoever things are lovely or of good report, if there be any virtue or praise, think on these things."

ONENESS OF ALL

When time has run its course where will you be? There are two places, 1. With Me, 2. Without Me. This is a true assessment of your future. There is a time of total separation forever of the lost ones. Right now all men are on earth, in earth, or in heaven, but when this time phase ends there will be just two places of men, the Lake of Fire or in Heaven with Me. Yes just two places because I will bring heaven and earth into a Oneness as all is My Heaven; the Universe and all that's in it. I will dwell on earth with man and We will have eternal Oneness of place and purpose, which is My plan, "The Oneness of All." Time is now growing more and more to be your enemy because of its shortness, your must take each hour more seriously because of its increasing worth to your future place with Me. Stir yourself up and wake up the lost ones NOW!

Lift your thinking beyond self. Imagine God is in His Heaven watching over you. He sees the beginning and the end. He has a plan for His world and for your life, and He is in charge. He has the power to do all things. However He knows what is best to bring His children to Himself. Because He has given everyone free will to choose, He must allow circumstances in lives to bring about their choosing God and not self or the worldly things. These lessons come into all lives and will be repeated until the lessons are learned. Be an over-comer and choose God's way. Let Him help you through, lean on Him in obedience and submission. Total surrender brings the joy of the Lord and peace in you heart. His over-flowing love will show the way!

ARE YOU READY?

My move toward the gathering of My children has been ongoing from the beginning, but now the happy results are just before Me. Oh how the Father has waited, anticipated, hoped, and desired this wonderful, beautiful time. Heaven and earth has been made in preparation for this event.

Like a great express train traveling down hill nothing can stop, hinder, alter, or change its course! There is the first [the first fruits are all ready gathered] great harvest just before Me and great tension is building on earth and in heaven. Vast assembling of collateral gatherings of support systems and background necessities. Oh what a tremendous effort is going into this one time, nothing ever like this harvest of souls will happen again in this size. Yes this first time will only be repeated in lesser degree once more. My assembling of My whole family is still stretched out over decades of time, but this first step is My greatest effort ever. Where are you now? Are you ready, eager, and watching?

Dwell in the presence of the Lord for it is there you will have the fullness of joy, and in His Glory is love and peace. As you walk in His presence, your life will be fulfilled. You will have the mind of Christ, as He will impart to you the knowledge necessary for your walk. "My God shall supply all your needs according to His riches in Glory through Jesus Christ." This word given to you becomes real as you dwell in His presence. Live in obedience and submission to receive the glorious blessings stored up for you. God's desire is to bless His children, but He can only do this when you are walking in His light. Trust and obey, walk always in His love and fulfill His plan for you. In His presence there truly is fullness of joy!

MY HEART

All of My plans and purposes for man have come from My heart of love to bless, and help, encourage, and guide My children into My arms forever. Love is the motivation of all I do, and I call all My children whose hearts are right for Me. I judge every man by his heart, I call every man in his heart, and I expect every man to give Me his whole heart. All of My efforts come from My heart to your heart. All My saved ones are saved when I give them a heart for Me. You must be found with a willing heart, seeking My way and Me. Only a heart such as I desire will I call into the family. Know this that all I do and all you do must come from a perfect heart! Speak to your hearts, call your heart perfect, and say, "My heart is perfect before My Heavenly Father." All who do this with a truthful willing heart are My children.

Allow God to reign in your heart! He is always with you but will you give Him first place? Let God truly direct your life through the unction of the Holy Spirit. The Holy Spirit is a glorious gift to you from your Heavenly Father. Acknowledge Him, listen to Him, heed and follow His direction for always it is for your good and for your Spiritual growth. The love of the Father abides in the Holy Spirit. All directions given are birthed out of love and mercy. "As many as are led by the Spirit of God, they are the sons of God." Be a true child of God and walk in the path shown to you by My Holy Spirit. It is a true walk of joy!

MY ARMY

My raising up an army of worth is only done when the individual soldiers are following Me with all of their heart, their time, and their prayers. An army has a life requirement, so does My Army! I require all their time, all their attention, and all of their hearts. When will I find soldiers like this? Where will I look but into your hearts, for it is in their hearts that I find true followers of worth. Dedication, obedience, attention, and time are all My requirements for My soldiers. I recruit those whose whole heart is given willingly, faithfully, and completely. I have no place for "Part Time" workers because the battle is never Part-Time. Come My dear ones can you reassess your place and position with Me honestly, truthfully, and can you say, "I am your soldier?" I gave My all, are you an "ALL Giver?"

Put your life in His hands, and know that you are a child of God. Live expecting the best, because God is your Heavenly Father. He created you and He loves you. Release that measure of faith that has been given you. Grow in faith, as God's word becomes a part of you. Engraft into your heart and soul the Word, the promises from the Father to His children. Let the power of the name of Jesus be released on your tongue. Remember you are joint-heirs with Jesus. Walk under the protection of His love and Glory by walking in love and obedience to the word, this is a path of Spiritual growth and great joy!

AS JESUS DID

When the devil comes against My children it only means they are not using the authority I've already given to them. When My Holy Spirit indwells My children greater is He that is in them than he that is in the world. Yes, My children have the authority and power available to do as Jesus did. Why don't they, because they all seem to wait for somebody else? When will one of them, then two of them, then a whole group of them rise up, rebuke and defeat the worthless lost of Satan's hordes. Come My dear ones, Jesus is here beside Me, but you He left on earth to finish the work and do His will. Are you not His Body still on earth, still living and alive in My Spirit? Rise up in the truth put right before you in My word, and in your heart, so let it penetrate into your mind making your body obedient. Let My will be done in you and through you. Speak out and see!

Walking in My presence brings forth manifold blessings. When We are walking together you are covered with My Glory and My protection. In this Glory is abundant love, peace, and joy in the Lord. When you are an open channel trusting Me I can impart to you the wisdom you desire and is necessary for your Spiritual growth. It is then that you are protected from the evil about you. Oh My children walk in the light, as I am the light. Let no darkness come neigh to you. Use the name of Jesus to help ward off the darkness. Let the light enfold you and permeate your being. For in this light is My eternal love. Believe and receive the abundant blessings I have for you!

A FACET OF LOVE

When the love of God flows out to man it is the release of God's Grace making it so! Grace is a facet of love that compels the heart of God to move in living action. Grace is a blinder God wears when the seeing of a thing would discourage Him. God's Heart, Love, and Grace are all parts of Him, giving expressions of His true self. This picture of God's Grace is given to show the children a direction they are going. It is the outgoing expressions, through Love and Grace, which will combine to make a man the Son of God. It is the flowing of Grace through Love that draws a man to God. Learn Love and Grace will flow, be gracious and Love will show. Do all things as unto the Lord, and wait upon the Lord to renew your strength, and then go forward knowing that all things are possible through Jesus Christ. Lean on Him for He is your source of all things. Walk in the path He has provided and the way will be made easy. Listen for the still small voice of the Holy Spirit. He is your guide and comforter, your helper in all your endeavors. My word tells you that "My yoke is easy and My burden is light." Believe this and let My love and My strength buoy you up. My Grace is sufficient for you. Together We can accomplish all things necessary for your Spiritual growth and you can truly be a light in this dark world. I am with you.

SEEK MORE

When will all of My children be able to see each other as I see them? Only when their Heart is cleansed and pure, only when My love is released through them in purity and truth. All of this is building now in every one of My obedient ones. Yes the growth of discipline and obedience is a slow work most of the time. Some come into a blessing quickly because they have been able to totally release self and this release gives way to My moving in their hearts without self's interference. This is the path all should follow, but it is not the path most travel. Seek more of My direction through listening and obeying the things I say. My word, the Bible, can be followed and the things I say there, or that I reveal through the word, can guide and direct, but it takes discipline and control that most children lack. When the Bible is taken in, as it should be, it opens up a way for Me to direct and help, but all growth depend on release of self's control.

Rise up and let the Holy Spirit be your guide. Overcome the physical heaviness. Let the power of the Holy Spirit be your strength. Lift your thinking to go to a higher plane where I can direct your thoughts and fill you with My love. As you wait on Me things will change. The darkness about you will flee and the light replace it. My love will flood your being and with it comes My joy. Walk constantly with praise on your lips that any evil may be broken up. Praise puts a barrier of protection all about you. Remember, you are a beloved child of God, joint-heirs with Jesus. Go forth with confidence that I am with you.

NO MAN IS WITHOUT

When the work of man is only self-centered then God has little use for him, when man's work becomes led by God's Holy Spirit then that same man can be taken to unbelievable heights. God's plans are so vast that no man is without immense potential with God. The walk taken by each child of God has never come to the perfection God has set and made available to each one. It is the willing obedience that opens the floodgates of blessings to each one of God's own. Only the truth seeking, self aborting children will ever know some of the things set before all of God's loved ones. Why aren't more children eager and striving to please God all of the time? Do you know? Do you seek more and more? Why not? Why not take the way of praise and thanksgiving, try that in every situation you have, the good and the bad!

All things come together in God's time. His plan is being fulfilled. Many lessons have to be learned before the end. Whatever comes upon you, use it as a growing experience. Do you let it overcome you or do you overcome it? Walk through life always growing Spiritually. Be confident that God's plan is being fulfilled. Have a thankful heart that He is with you and you are progressing from one level to the next. Go through each lesson knowing "You can do all things through Christ who strengthens you." You are not alone. His Glory and love are imparted to you as needed when you are one with your Lord and Savior. Allow Him to be your guide and your strength. He is able!

DAILY DESIRE

The things I bring to My children are daily, but not all of them will be listening and paying attention. My call on their life is a permanent one, but they make it so haphazard that I wonder why I call, most do not listen! To bring My love to each child of Mine is My daily desire, but too few are available. I seek My will and way to be done each day but there are so few listening. The times ahead are demanding My attention and way be done, and only the few will be available, why is that? Do you know? Test your heart this day, right now, and let's face each other in loving truth. Do you love Me? Do you care for all I've done for you? Wake up now and let's do the final task together!

Receive all God has for you; remember you have been cleansed by the blood of Jesus Christ. You have been given the gift of the Holy Spirit so your body is a temple of God's Spirit. Therefore, "Arise shine, for the light is come and the Glory of the Lord is risen upon you." Let this light shine that others may see Jesus in you. Be a constant source of love, of kindness, and peace to all around you. Be confident of God's presence in your life, "Supplying all your needs according to His riches in Glory."

THEIR PURPOSES, MY PURPOSE

In the training of My loved ones, I find a great divergence of attention from them. This is interesting to Me because it gives Me opportunity to explore each one's true desires and purposes, and to separate their purposes and My purpose for them becomes a challenge. How much quicker and simpler it would be if all My children would come to Me in a simple open honest way. However the sorting of self's push from love's tugs, love for Me not for self, is what I have given each man time in the flesh to sort out. The end result will figure perfectly into My overall plan for man's place in My eternity. You must understand every one of My children have a major part to play in the decisions of where and what kind of eternal position they will have in the kingdom of God. No one can ever think later on that I was just playing favorites. This is why there will be perfect harmony in Heaven, all will know they were the ones who choose their place of forever!

In all things look to God for He is your source, and let His love and peace flood your soul, then your strength will be renewed, your questions answered, and your needs provided. To walk in His love, His presence brings about fulfillment. In His Glory you are One with Him. Rise above the problems of the day by allowing the fullness of the Lord to envelope you and sustain you. In prayer and praise, with a thankful heart, draw close to Him. Take of the power of the Holy Spirit within you, and let the Holy Spirit be the leader in your life. "He who is led by the Holy Spirit is the son of God." This is the desire of the Father's heart.

REACH THE HEIGHTS

It is the continuing in My will and way that will raise My children up to the stature of My Son Jesus. Yes, He is your example in all things that I call you to. He has made adequate provision for every child of Mine to reach the heights of Heavenly awareness necessary to fulfill My heart's desire for each and everyone I draw to Me. Walk in this knowledge daily knowing who you are in Christ, because when your believing is consistent and compelling then I can draw and complete Our work of perfection you require. This is your path of true believing that will bring you Godly achieving.

Each day the important thing is to walk with Me in My presence. This will lift you up out of the worldly cares and out of thoughts of self. Choose constantly to do My will and overrule self. The physical, or self, is at war with the Spiritual and you must choose the path you will take. Lessons are learned by the choices you make. Make your affirmation, "Today I choose to walk continually in God's presence, I choose love, peace, and joy," He is your Heavenly Father and your Creator. Be the child of God He intended you to be, "In the fullness of joy!"

THE DESIRE

It is when I give release that My children can begin a work for Me. When, you ask, will I give the release? Only when hearts are prepared and I find them ready and acceptable! Study to show yourself prepared. Just reading the Bible doesn't make you ready; it's just a start! Your heart must have the desire to know My things and that knowing must become a search for My truth. When My truth is your goal then I can use a truth seeker for My purposes. Yes, the main and best thing to start with is seeking the truth behind My words. In this way Our will is cemented into your new Spirit and We can then become One in love, truth, and trust! True love will pursue truth because true love only reveals truth. All truth is a revelation on love, but all love is too much for all truth to show!

Today is a special day in the Lord. It is a day to draw closer to Him, to receive all He has for you, to bask in the Glory of His love. Let yourself receive the blessings stored up for you in My Spirit. As your comforter and helper I stand ready to uplift you, and strengthen you, and give you a gloriously happy heart as you experience a measure of the love of the God. My children put self behind you and reach out for the Glories of the Lord. Anticipate and expect the very best in your life. Walk in praise and thanksgiving with your eyes on the Lord. His eyes are on you constantly in love and with a desire to help, to teach you the lessons necessary for your Spiritual growth. Everything you need is available in your Heavenly Father.

ROAD OF CERTAINTY

When will you become just what I wish you to be? First, no one knows but the Father. Second, there is a start, a release that only you can give. Third, to "become" is already in process, and to be is already in Our hands. This path is a road of certainty only when you make the right moves. You are your own savior because Jesus only saves those who are drawn by the Father, and He only draws those who's hearts are seeking, that comes back to Him! All are saved by and because Jesus prepared the path back to the Father, but the teamwork part is "No one comes to the Father unless the Holy Spirit draws them." Now when will you become just what I wish you to be, "That's the question and the answer still is the same as the salvation question. When will you give up self, and seek and desire with all your heart to become just what I wish you to be? You release, We draw further, you give up more, and We draw you closer. This has nothing to do with your salvation, which happens first, and from then on it's a trip to bring you where I wish you to be!

"Thou will keep him in perfect peace, whose mind is stayed on thee." It is especially important now to remember and act upon these words. There is confusion and upset in the world, but the Father has peace and love and joy prepared for His chosen ones. Decide whom you will serve today, self or your Heavenly Father. In God's way is enlightenment and peace of mind. In His plan He walks beside you. If you choose self, you walk alone. His Glory can enfold you and lift you up to Heavenly places. Let His love be your guide and you will be fulfilled and made complete. The work that God began in you He will finish. Praise the Lord!

A GOOD QUESTION

Each day has the time allotted that will lift you closer to Me; this is what each day is to be used for. I give you each day, isn't it reasonable that you would want to find out why? My dear ones isn't this a good question? If you would rise early in the morning, and sit and wait upon Me, couldn't We reason this thing out? Maybe I will show you something in My word just for your use today, and later, maybe I could bring you a new revelation about your work, or your family, or maybe something I want you to do, don't you want that? How will you ever know if all written here is even for you? Don't you want to know? All this is just a guide and help to My obedient ones, is that you?

The Glory of the Lord covers the earth, and His Glory, His Light, is all about you and available to all. If there is darkness in your life it is because self is totally in charge and you have chosen the wrong path. The path the Lord has prepared for you is one of Spiritual growth, with love, peace, and joy to sustain and lift you up. Follow the path set forth by the Holy Spirit. "He who is led by My Spirit is My Son." As trials and temptations come, go through them holding Jesus' hand, confident that Spiritual lessons are being learned. Keep an attitude of a quiet Spirit, in peace, knowing that you are not alone. Your Abba Father is with you, and His Spirit and love are protecting you from the onslaught of the evil one. You are being carried through if you lean on Him. Trust and obey knowing," All is Well."

RIGHT NOW

The daily working with My children is My wish and plan, but when will all of My children daily work with Me? I call, I seek, I draw, I pursue, but where are all My children? Where will they be at the trumpet blast? You who know Me answer this last call, "Save My Lost Ones." Now is the time, now right where you are, look around, don't you see the lost ones all around you? Do you say hello to them? Do you tell them I'm coming very, very soon? Do you care? I'm trying to wake you up, so you'll wake them up, so I can take you all up! Come and do this last great work. Your task is not hidden; your call is not secret. Have I not just said what I desire for you to be doing? Be My voice right where you are, right now today!

Right now take hold of the joy and the peace that is available to you through Jesus Christ. Experience the great love of your Savior by keeping your eyes on Jesus. Anticipate good things in your life because you are a child of God. "I would that you prosper and be in good health as you soul prospers," God's holy words to you. Your soul prospers by soaking it in the word of God and by having a heart of praise and thanksgiving.

Seek the face of Jesus and be led by the Holy Spirit within. Lean on the Lord constantly for He is able to sustain you and carry you through all lessons necessary for your Spiritual growth. God's love will prevail and He shall direct your path. Choose victory in Jesus!

SURE CERTAINTY

There is to come a great opportunity opening up, a time of My plans being shown clearly to each child of Mine. This will be a time of truth, making each one responsible for his own actions, exposing clearly each ones plan for his life with Me. Here will be the time of decision making that will set each one's place in eternity with a sure certainty. This is early notice to each one who reads this note: look for, be ready, and eagerly grasp this gift from the Father. This will open up your path, as never before, this will show you clearly your planned way with the Father. To know this is also a gift of helps so more of God's children will find their own place in the Father's plan. Don't you look for, and desire to know, just what you'll be doing for and with the Lord?

With a humble Spirit go forward in God's plan, this will help keep self from being dominant, because in living for self and selfish desires is death to the Spirit. Rise above this by keeping your eyes on Jesus, your lips full of praise, and your feet on the path that has been prepared for you. As a child of God you are joint-heirs with Jesus. Your loving Heavenly Father will not allow more trials and tribulations to come upon you than you can bear. He is truly your protection and your burden bearer, if you lean on Him. "Cast your cares on Him for He cares for you." Walk freely knowing your strength and guidance are from the Lord.

MY CALL

When I call I always have a purpose, do you hear the call? Do you seek the purpose? Are you sure We are together in all things? My dear ones I call and many do not hear, why is that? Is that you? Why must My calls go unanswered? Now you, who are reading this, know that My call is in your heart, in your spirit-self, it is within you, and you must hear Me. How can you hear if you are never quiet? How can you hear Me when your mind is always occupied with cares of the world or just plain entertainment? I give you your time, so can't you be still and listen for My call sometime? This appeal is vital to Our growing together, so I'm making My plea now, in this time and place, because I love you. Won't you listen more for My call?

God's light [His word is to enlighten you] is available to all His children. You are free to choose the light or darkness. If the Spirit is leading you, you will be living in the light and overcome self, which usually walks in darkness. There is joy in the light, and in the love of the Lord. "In His presence is fullness of joy." In His presence you become a doer of the word, not just a hearer. There is joy in caring for others, in giving to the Lord or to those who are in need, or being compassionate to all God's children. Walk in the light for, "God is light, and in Him is no darkness at all." Walk in the light so you may have life more abundantly.

FILTERED WORDS

When all is settled then will My truth appear in its completeness. All My children will know and understand completely the words I speak to them. They are now able to hear only filtered words in their hearts, but at the release of truth, all truth will burst forth, and then there will be such a revelation that the Heavens will ring with such singing and joy filled sounds of splendid wonder such as has never before been released. Keep this promise always in front of your mind and heart, and you will find the blessings of its anticipation bringing you rewarding thoughts of pleasant desire.

Use this time given to you to be a reflection of God's love. You are His hands and feet, and His voice of love ministering to others. Fill your heart with His perfect love, and let it be seen in your words and actions. Rise above self and the pull of the world, and make an effort, and the Lord will do the rest. You are an over-comer with God's help. His Glory will sustain you in all your works for Him. Think love, think compassion, and think forgiveness, and wonders will be accomplished. Let your soul be led by the wonderful Holy Spirit in sweet submission, and you will be complete and fulfilled in His presence.

SO THEY MAY KNOW

The work of man for himself must be exposed as a useless endeavor, because it only continues their fall into wastefulness. God has a place and a plan for every one of His children. When you speak to the lost children make this point a strong one. Stop pleasing "self" and seek to please God the Creator of all men. "Soul saving" is the banner and call most important in these last few days. Wake up the lost and stir up their hearts by your appeal to their good senses. Tell them what Jesus did for them, tell them they are not lost but found! Tell them Jesus loves them, tell them, and tell them so they may know!

Tell them to: Rejoice for the Son has set you free, and you are free indeed. You have been freed from your sins, past, present, and future. You have been freed from the cares of the world for He said; "Cast your cares on Me for I care for you." You have His peace, "My peace I give you." God has bestowed strength upon you if you, "Wait upon the Lord and renew your strength." God planned for you to have an abundant life through life with Him. His word promises, "My God shall supply all your needs according to His riches in Glory." Receive the wonderful blessings promised, walk in His presence at all times, and you will have fullness of joy, so rejoice My children, rejoice!

LOVING WALK

When will I be able to display all of My plans before you, to show you things to come, show you where We are going, and bring you to the things that you desire on your walk with Me. Yes, I am waiting for the release from you showing Me your complete trust. You must come to that time of knowing when your giving up of self is complete, and We have entered into a new, open, more loving daily walk. All things will become new, old friends will see changes in relationship, and love will be easier and more apparent with everyone. There is a time just ahead when things on earth will be more like things in heaven, just as you have prayed so often.

Take of My love, and My mercy, and fill your soul with the blessings it brings. Immerse yourself in the love of God, and obedience will follow. My will, will be made clear, as you put on the mantle of love. For I am love and all things are made perfect in love. As you walk in My presence, the precious agape love will be imparted to you. You are to be a channel of this blessing, allowing it to flow to all others that they may know Me, and know My blessings in their lives. Have the mind of Christ, have the compassion and mercy of Christ, and have the love so freely given to the children of God. They will truly know you are Christians by your love.

WHAT TO DO

There should always be meaningful purpose to each day given to you, My loved ones in worthless pursuits waste too many days. What should I be doing you ask Me? Well that question would be the right one to bring to Me each morning. Can't you see the wisdom of that way? Yes, dear ones, ask Me about each day, come to Me for counsel and I will give you wisdom and encouragement for your efforts. Our walk during these next few days will set a place of great worth for you, when your purposes become My purposes for each of your days. This is the prime time of learning for all who will listen, and hearing will obey and do. Doing the way and will of the Lord is now the only way for My listening ones, where is your heart? It should be where the "ears of your heart" are, always open to My words!

Walk upright for you are an over-comer. Keep your eyes on the Lord and not on the problems at hand. Wait upon the Lord and your strength will be renewed, your mind cleared, and everything will come into focus. Be not bent down by the problems of the physical. You are Spirit, and the Holy Spirit leads you. The restoration comes through the Holy Spirit to your Spirit, and then penetrates through the soul and body. When you wait upon the Lord this saturation is taking place, this filling of God's Glory and love, which restores all things but an attitude of belief and trust is necessary. Believe the healing scriptures, and claim them for your own. God's promises are for you. Be the over-comer He wants you to be!

SO FEW

When will all My children walk and talk what I've already put in their hearts? Only when they have set their Spirit to take charge, and not be led by their feelings and flesh desires. My Holy Spirit I've given to be their guide, teacher, and helper, but so few really pay Him much attention. My word, the Bible, along with My Spirit opening up their understanding, will be sufficient to meet all of their needs. Call on Me and I will answer, seek Me and I will be found, but it is not a hit or miss approach that will find Me, only My dedicated, submitted, seeking Ones will ever find My path for them. Open your Spiritual eyes to see truth, seeking Me every day, not hit or miss, but all of the time, what better do you really have than that?

Walk in the light as He is in the light, and humble yourself in the sight of the Lord and He will lift you up. As you humble yourself, wait upon the Lord until the light shows you the direction God has planned for you. There is a perfect plan for you filled with God's Glory, love, peace, and joy. All these blessings are waiting for you. Walk in peace as the Holy Spirit is leading you. Doing His will instead of your own will, will produce joy in your life. Remember, "God will supply all your needs according to His riches in Glory." Be an over comer and rise above every obstacle with the help of the Father. He will truly complete what He has begun in your life.

VICTORY IS ASSURED

It is the determination in the heart of My children to overcome the flesh and self that will be their salvation over the earth and its ways. With that kind of response I can then support, encourage, lead, and guide them into My planned walk for each of them. Victory is assured every struggling body, soul, and spirit that I've found to be seeking truth in My earth place that I have put him or her. No one is ever lost whose heart is found seeking truth, I always know them, and always guide them into My loving arms. However their salvation is also in the hands of My saved ones, and I require that all should seek to save the lost. No matter where you are, My children, you are to seek and save My lost children. This is the last and greatest time of salvation covering the whole earth and reaching all the lost wherever they are. Are you a part of My plan?

Let go and let God do the things for you He has promised in His word. He said, "My peace I give you, not as the world gives, give I to you." Let go of the turmoil in your life and receive this peace. "I have come that you may have life, and that more abundantly." Are you living in life abundantly? Are you walking in health? "He sent His word and healed them." Receive your abundance and your healing for you are a child of God, and He is truly a God of love. With a humble spirit receive all that your Heavenly Father has for you. Walk daily in His grace and in the power of His love!

A GIFT OF LIFE

The ongoing tasks of life are not intended to hinder or stop My children from drawing close to Me each day. Each day is a gift of life I give, and these days of earth blessings are to prepare all My loved ones to come to Me. No work of man should ever interfere with their pursuit of My ways and Me. Come dear ones and do the things of necessity only to maintain, and then give the proper time and attention to My requirements and Me. If you do this with diligence and sincerity of heart then I can make your way more pleasant and profitable. Just give Me time in the early morning and take Me on your daily walk, and then you will see and know how much I love you and how much I can help you.

You are a part of the Bride of Christ. You have this lifetime to prepare yourself for the joining, or the wedding, to the Lamb of God, Jesus Christ. It is to be a heart preparation, your saved Spirit wooing and winning the soul and body into submission, and walking with Jesus in love. You have My help [Holy Spirit] to be your helper and comforter. I will lead you into the ways of righteousness, if you will forget self and follow My Lord. The word is your guide; the love of the Lord is your strength and your shield. God is always with you when your heart is open to Him. Be an over comer, keep your eyes on the Lord, and persevere for the time is short. The rewards are glorious. Walk in His love and be the victor He desires you to be!

MY WAY

If every day you have were given to Me, and you put yourself at My disposal, then We could see great and wonderful results. For My way would become clearer to you each day, and I could direst your walk in the paths you should go. This is My plan for you, and I then would have you as My close companion. Who knows how far We could go? I know and I desire that My way be revealed to you more every day. Only by giving Me your time and attention can I ever draw you into the perfection I have for you. Submission begins each morning when We come together. Obedience occurs as your listening and hearing improves and you become a doer. Oh My children this call of Mine, day after day, is for your blessing and benefit so We can become a blessing and benefit to the lost children. All of Our efforts should now be the saving of the lost souls the Father is still seeking.

Open up your heart and take more of Me. By allowing more of Me and My righteousness to fill your soul, you are diminishing self and the ways of the world. There is no room for darkness when light comes in. In this manner the fruit of the Spirit is released into your being and you will be flooded with My love, joy, and peace. With these blessings come patience, goodness, faith, meekness, and self-control. My children let the potential, which is yours from Me, blossom in your life. You will experience joy evermore and overcome every obstacle.

YOUR CROSS

When I say pick up your cross I am speaking of things in the Spirit, I stayed on the cross until all of My soul and spirit were under perfect control, and then I released My only tie with the Father, only then was I totally committed to do the work of the Father. Your cross is handled in the same spirit of truth. You carry your self burdens daily until you find the time and place of the cross where you too can let go of your self and come into the fire of perfection with Me. Not all of My loved ones can come in the flesh to this place of release, but many have and many will until the time of final gathering. There is much work that I am doing in the Spirit realm, which My children are never aware of, nevertheless the work proceeds around My loved ones all of the time.

Praise and worship Almighty God, the Creator of all things. He is also your loving heavenly Father. He created you and knew you before you were born. He created you in love, and has a plan for your place in the family of God. Take advantage of this earth time to learn the lessons necessary for your Spiritual growth. This time on earth is to prepare the children of God to be with Him in eternity. You must learn to be led by the Holy Spirit, and to read and know My word. The promises there are for you, as is the instructions for living a Godly life. My commandments are just, and will bring freedom and righteousness to your life. Lean on the Lord; trust Him to lead the way. His love will smooth the way. Let the joy of the Lord be your strength and you will walk in victory!

GREAT ANTICIPATION

When I give a call to a child of Mine, that call is not the only call I'll give. I want the communication more than most of them. So I'll keep on calling and waiting. Why is it that I would have to wait? Why wouldn't each child of Mine be eager and waiting, looking for and seeking My call with great anticipation? Is this a thing so rare as to be unbelievable? Why would that be? What must I do to wake up the sleeping, lazy, and too busy ones? These times are fast disappearing, never to be like this again. This time of My last great gathering is also a special time of revelation, communication, and growing closer than ever before! Today this is a note to wake up everyone that will read this, come into Our private place and time each morning, and learn more about your way I would have you go.

Rejoice for the time draws near when I will take you home with Me to live forever in heaven. You are in the earth but you are not of the earth. Use this time on earth to grow Spiritually, learn to overcome and draw closer to Me. In all things seek My face by letting go and let God, then follow the lead of the Holy Spirit and He will bring you into My righteousness. Walk always in My presence and My love will sustain you. In My love is strength, peace of mind, and joy divine. Walk in this joy that I give, which truly fills the soul with My blessings. Together We are victors, so persevere and remember, "All is well."

SPOKEN WITH LOVE

I am giving to you words of wisdom, words the Father desires you to use, to bring light and understanding to everyone who is called My child. These words are building blocks for life everlasting; they will open up new life and bring joy and peace out of earth's turmoil. My words, spoken through My servants, will have all the purpose and power as if I had said them. To be a true, clear, conveyor of My words is a privilege I give, as I desire, not to all or everyone do I give this honor, but to everyone I say listen, heed, and hear what My prophet say. My words are all powerful, filled with purpose, spoken in love, and sent out to fulfill My desire. Make only careful analysis of My words for they are My thoughts expressed in perfection to bring health, help, healing, and love. To properly receive My words with understanding is to be blessed by Me!

Rest assured that, "The good work God began in you, He will perform until the day of Jesus Christ." His plans will come to fruition whether you are a willing child of God or a stumbling block. Learn the lesson through the circumstances that come upon you. Keep your eyes on the Lord for He has the answers, He has the wisdom, the patience, and the strength. It is not what happens to you that is important, but how you react to it! Your attitude through it all determines your Spiritual growth. Thus patience is so important as is a loving attitude toward others. Can you have a heart of compassion? Can you react as Jesus would? Can you have the mind of Christ as you go through life's problems? You can if your mind is stayed on Him.

PURPOSE FULFILLED

It is not with everyone I can give My words to because I know the inconsistency of men. However, with some I have faith that what I give them will be properly used, respected, and then it will accomplish that for which it was given. To keep this gift alive is a blessing to be honored, and then there is to be much purpose fulfilled when such worthiness flows. To keep on a path once it has been given requires a willingness of service that will build a storehouse of plenty. To receive My word is one thing, to make My word live is another thing, but to spread My words becomes a wealth of good that moves endlessly to My purpose. Keep on keeping on, all is well.

I would that you take the joy of the Lord to this unhappy world. You, who have the indwelling Spirit, rise up and let the light of Jesus shine through you. There is joy in knowing Jesus as your Lord and Savior. Express this joy in your daily life. Be the light and the salt of the earth that the Lord planned for you to be. Overcome the trials and tribulations in your life by having a heart and compassion for others. Have a caring attitude toward all others, and see them through the eyes of Jesus with love. What can you do today to show forth God's love? God is love and you are a child of God. Do they know you are a Christen by your love?

A SHORT TIME SET

The things I bring for you each morning are an outpouring of My love for all of My children. For this effort to be properly used I will set My word on high. My words will not be wasted, lost, buried or set aside, but My words will be sent to all nations, tribes, and people. My words are powerful, and filled with loving guidance and I will not have them wasted, lost, buried or mis-used! There is a short time set for the release of My books, and then I will follow them wherever they go, and I will make these words of Mine alive in the hearts of all of My children. No matter where, I will find a place and a time for My words to work to their greatest advantage. No time with My words will be lost, no time in the using or the application of My words will they not be watched over, led, and guided by My Spirit, servants, and helpers. Take heart in all you are doing, keep on keeping on!

The flesh wars against the Spirit. You are to be led by the Holy Spirit, operating through your Spirit. Your Spirit has been renewed; you are a new man in Christ Jesus. Therefore put down the flesh [the old man] and let the Spirit lead the way. "Greater is He that is in you than he that is in the world." That includes Satan and the flesh. As a new man there is more power in the Spirit than in Satan, the flesh, or self. Call on this power of God given to you. Be an over-comer, put down self and worldly thoughts, and let the Holy Spirit direct your path. It is the path God has chosen for you, the way of righteousness filled with love. Walk daily in the presence of the Lord and receive the fullness of joy He has for you!

TIME NO MORE

When will all of the hearts of all of My people belong to Me? When will I reign forever in the places that I have chosen? When will all of My children know Me in all of My beauty, wonder, and strength? When will time be no more, and hours and minutes are gone? When will I see all about Me complete and perfect, as I am perfect? When will all of these things come to pass? *Only when all of the hearts of all of My people belong to Me!* Oh My dear ones keep on the way I have shown you, keep your hearts close to Me, you can do all I ask, when I ask, because it is what I ask, and you can do all I ask! How can you do all I ask? By My love, My dear ones there is power in My love I have not spoken about to you, because you must prepare your hearts properly to not only receive the knowledge of love, but you must understand the power of love. This power will be released at the final gathering time. I am mentioning it to you now because this is the beginning of the preparation of the hearts of My children for My release of love in power and strength. All opposition will fall at this release; all plans will be set at the final end of this age. Love will control and move as The Father has ordained, and all plans will be released for Our final earth acts.

In your prayer life think as a child of God. My family is spread around the world, so consider your brothers and sisters in Christ in all parts of the world. Consider the areas where darkness prevails. Could you let some of God's light in by your fervent prayers? Be mindful of My children, who know not of Me, or the blessings I have for them. My children, your prayers make a difference. "The effectual fervent prayers of a righteous man availith much." Let the compassion of the Lord fill your heart. Have mercy in your prayers and My promise to you is "it will make a difference."

THE GIFT GIVEN

It is the ongoing work of love that My children must let continue and grow. Yes, My love is to grow and grow. The only purpose I put in every child of Mine that is exactly the same is "To spread My love." Yes, every child of Mine that is called has the basic call to spread My love abroad as I have done in My Son. To follow Jesus in all the work I give you will not progress properly unless it progresses basically through love. It is My love given that is the one common gift every child of Mine has. To claim that gift of love, and be moved by that gift of love, will become the precious tool of motivation propelling My work to perfect completion. Come My dear ones and pray for, seek, desire, and believe for this love in you to spread as wildfire in a forest!

"For God so loved the world that He gave His only begotten Son." Love is the key factor. God is Love. As His children, He expects you to walk in love, "Agape Love" His love! Be aware of His presence, His Glory, and His perfect love about you at all times. Act out of this love. See others through the love of Jesus. God's love acts as a protection about you, your shield from evil. It brings the peace that passes understanding in a world of chaos. Walk in that love, that peace, and be the light of the world a child of God should be! Draw on what is available to you through that power of the Holy Spirit, love, peace, and joy. These are gifts from your loving Heavenly Father. Receive them and know the joy of His presence.

JUBILEE TIME

When all of My work for this time is completed there will be a Jubilee Time of loving expression that will touch the hearts of all of My children together. There will be such Oneness of being moving among Us that man has never felt before; it is an expression of the Father's love held until this special time. Angels have never known or seen such a thing, only in God's heart has this been pondered over the ages. Oh, what an experience of sweeping, penetrating, all abiding, love touching the hearts of everyone called God's children. My dear ones while this is just a note of encouragement it is also a further revealing of truth of the Father's love for all of you. Keep this kind of note always near your heart, it will bring healing, help, and encouragement for the times ahead.

As you work your way through the stumbling blocks, or rocks, that block your way on the path of righteousness, they become as pebbles. Then in perseverance, with God's help, the pebbles are broken up and become sand. As you struggle through, much is being accomplished in your Spiritual life. Keep on keeping on, with your eyes on the Lord, and walking in His guidance. All is well with your soul. Let each day be a step closer in your walk with your Heavenly Father. He sees your struggle and is always there to lift you up. Take joy in His love that surrounds you and keep your eyes on the goal ahead, Oneness with God and your blessed Savior Jesus Christ.

A REACHABLE BLESSING

With each day, I bring you there is a blessing that you can reach for, do you know what that is each day? Only by drawing closer to Me in the reality of Our Oneness will you ever find out what I'm talking about. Yes this is a true statement, why wouldn't it be? I'm always with you, are you always with Me in awareness? I'm very aware of you, I am watching over you and I'm now asking if you are reciprocating this loving attention? Come dear ones and hear what I'm saying, hear it in your heart, bring this reality into perfect focus because We must have a closer walk now. Your future with Me can be greatly enhanced by the attention and changes I can bring to help you grow into the person I plan for you to be. I have a wonderful concept of what you are becoming, and I have the desire to make it so, but it will only happen when you are doing the things that I will help you do.

Cry unto the Lord, and your help will come upon you. Keep in constant communication with your Heavenly Father. He is waiting to hear from you His beloved children. His eye is upon you, but He has given you free will. You are free to call upon Him or do it yourself. You are free to choose God or self, so in all things turn to your God for He is the answer. His way is the way. There are blessings for you on His path, and even Spiritual growth and peace in your heart. God hears your prayers and answers in love. Walk this life's path holding His hand. Let Him guide you in all things.

YOUR SOURCE

There are many children chosen and many children blessed but I have just a few that I can lead and guide daily. It is a blessing to Me to have such children! God is your source of all things, so Let joy and peace flood your soul, as you trust in and lean on Him. He is Almighty God, and He desires that you walk the path He has prepared for you that you may grow Spiritually into a Oneness with Him. He is always available, watching over you, waiting for you to look to Him in all things. See your faith build as He responds to your prayers. Know that in Him "All is Well." Have a heart for others and spread abroad the love, and peace, and joy that you receive from your Lord. He is truly your source!"

NOTE OF AWAKENING

It is with great power and strength that I cause all My children to be drawn closer to Me each day. Should they waste all of that through their lack of paying Me the proper attention? This is a note of great importance. My children have only a limited time left for them to be gathered in the perfection I have planned for them. It is their last time of great Spiritual awakening. This word is a "great awakening" word and their, each individual's, eternal life will profit greatly by the attention and obedience they give to Me in these times. Have no doubt about what is here said! My dear ones you must come to this time right now with all of your heart, mind, soul, and body given freely to your Holy Spirit. He has, within each of you, all that you need to fulfill My greatest desires for you. Listen; hear with your heart's ears, for the truth He will be giving to you. You must give Him all the time He needs from now on, because these are your very last times to grow and attain all of this earth's victory the Father desires for you!

"My word is a light unto your path." Keep My word constantly in your heart, in your thoughts, and on your lips. It will become a way of life if you persevere. My word changes things from selfish thoughts of self and the world to happy thoughts from Me of love, peace, and joy! As you praise the Lord your attitude will change and you will allow the windows of heavens to be opened with blessings pouring out. Praise concentrates your being on thanking the Heavenly Father. "I will bless the Lord at all times, His praise shall continually be in my mouth." It will change your life and give joy to your Father in Heaven.

WALK OF COMPLETION

No man has ever given to Me all that I have asked of him, yet I still have found great and mighty men with Me. It is only as I call and raise up these ones, can I have a walk of completion for Jesus. My call is on each and every child who will hear, and hearing will pay attention and then obey. Our walk together is not dependent upon Me. Our walk is only dependent upon the children who I call! Every child is equal in My eyes and I am blessed with each one as they respond the best way they know how. Only the ones who give Me their whole heart are the ones I can give high positions and places of authority in My Kingdom. All of My children are Kingdom Kids, but all will not be leaders. This note is to help each one of you to understand, I do not give out worthy positions easily or carelessly. If any are blessed with high places in My Kingdom, it will be through their release of self and obedience to all I ask.

Put Jesus first in life, and all things will work together for good. He is your source of all things; health, finances, peace of mind, protection, and knowledge. Walk in the path He has set before you, keeping your eyes on Him. Jesus is your advocate with the Heavenly Father. He is your example of love. Keep His Commandments of Love, and all will be well for you. To love God, know you are filled with His love, and you are to be to be a channel of that agape love to all others, to do so is to fulfill all of the commandants. Love covers a multitude of sins. God is your source of love, so open your hearts and receive all He has to give. Walk in His presence for "In His presence is fullness of joy."

ULTIMATE GOAL

All of man's imaginations are not wrong or bad; I can bring many of My children closer to Me if I control this kind of their thought life. My children are to give to Me all of their life, all of their hopes, all of their dreams, and then I can give a clean vessel all of My love, all of My care, and all of My attention. The life I give each one is only to please and satisfy My plan for their Forever. Failure to release self, and give their life fully to Me, will bring every lost one to eternal disaster. It is by receiving Christ in their hearts that I can bring perfection "Forever" to all who I call, and I will bless, love, lead, and guide every child of Mine into a forever place of wonderful love. Love is the ultimate goal of Forever!

Never doubt the faithfulness of the Lord. His Glory is ever lasting and covers everything. His love is about each of His children, protecting and sustaining them. Be aware of His presence in your life. Keep praise and worship on your lips in an attitude of thanksgiving. Know His word and claim His promises to you. There are promises of health, of supply, and of peace of mind. Think of the promise, "I will never leave you nor forsake you." His love and mercy covers all His children, and all situations that may arise. Have an attitude of joy and thanksgiving because you are a child of God, a joint-heir with Jesus. In all things give thanks for He desires that you live abundantly.

DAILY VISIT

The daily visit with each of My loved ones is a constant blessing to all of Us. We are equally involved in each child of Ours. Our lives with Our children are to be an everlasting, ongoing, continuous time forever. We have plans that are continually unfolding. The Father is a never-ending source of loving care and activity, which will always bless, encourage, and bring great joy. All of this flows unstoppable from the Love of the Father, Who is Himself an ever ongoing, always loving resource that never runs dry. My dear children of My great Kingdom keep forever this picture I send you today because truth is an everlasting blessing to be kept a permanent fixture in your heart of hearts!

Each day is another stepping stone in your Spiritual growth. Whatever comes, be an over-comer by having and attitude of praise ad thanksgiving. Let joy and peace fill your heart as you anticipate the blessings of the Father falling upon you. He is with you, I, the Holy Spirit, am leading you and the Savior Jesus Christ is your advocate. Knowing this, as promised in the Word, you are protected. "There shall no evil befall you." Therefore walk in confidence, pouring forth God's Agape Love. This is His desire for you. Be a light in this dark world. Show forth the victory in your life through Jesus Christ.

CONSISTENT LOVE

In all I say and all I do there is a consistent love flowing. I operate from a high position, and I operate from a low position. Position does not dictate what I say or do. Only The Father of all Glory is the source of everything, and I move and have My being to serve and do all that The Father desires. My position is an Always Place with the One of All. All of the children of the Kingdom are in a growing place of Oneness Forever. This is the Father's plan, and it is a display of perfection the like of which has never been before and will never be again. Only the children of Forever will be the perfect result of all The Father has set up to be. Keep this picture of your Oneness with The Father of All, because your future joy and happiness stems from only One Source. Love is your birthplace, Love is your home, Love is your comfort, and Love is your forever place of rest.

"They that wait upon the Lord shall renew their strength." Let the strength and peace of Jesus flow into your being as you rest in Him. There is a time to stop busy activities and take of the peaceful blessings of the Lord. Meditate on Him that your soul may be restored. Quiet the body that God may renew your strength. Remember, "Be still and know that I am God." Anticipate and expect to be renewed, do not dwell on the weaknesses, they are a passing thing. Expect the abundant life that God has promised His children, and you shall walk in victory. "Peace, be still for I am with you."

LOVING CARE

It is the day-by-day task of all My children to seek My face and call on My name, then draw close for Our daily walk. All of your day is still before you leaving the time and place for Us to go. When will each one put this time in My hands, and seek My guidance, and listen to My loving care? I will bring the right events about to lead and guide all you do, this is the way to be blessed day by day! Will you give this day to Me, all day? If you do I will come through! Don't let your blessings be missed, and don't let the blessings others could have from Me be lost! Come let's take a walk!

Go forth boldly, for you walk in the way of the Holy Spirit. You are a child of God. "For as many as are led by the Spirit of God, they are the sons of God." The Holy Spirit leads you through the lessons, and you are to learn to grow Spiritually. He protects and keeps you safe. He fills your heart with peace and joy. He shows you the higher way, God's way to live your life. You are free to choose God's way or your way. Choose God's will and you will reap the blessings He has stored up for you. His love surrounding you will make all things possible. In Him you are a victor!

HEAVENLY WONDERS

I know all the thoughts and hopes that are in the hearts and minds of My children, still I love them, and seek to draw them into a closer walk with

Me each day. I do not see failures, I see steps of growth, and I do not see lies and deceit, but struggles of the lost ones. I do not look for their errors, but for their hopes and true desires of their heart. Oh how I long to sit down with each one of My children every morning and just tell them I'm real and true, just tell them to come closer to Me each day, and then I'll direct their path into My heavenly wonders of love and hope. The truth lies in what I say; don't you want to hear truth each morning? Don't you really want to walk on My path of love each day? Come My dear ones and let Us be together more in the mornings.

Be led by the Holy Spirit, and live in peace, listening for that sweet soft voice of God's Spirit living within you. He is the voice of God, and was given to you to be your comforter, and helper. He is your seal of redemption, put within you as a promise of your eternal life with Him. Appreciate the fruit of the Spirit, readily available to you at all times. Call on the blessings of the Spirit, release them and make them a part of your life. Show forth in your life what has been given you; love, peace, joy, patience, gentleness, goodness, faith, meekness, and self-control. These precious gifts from the Father are yours to release and share with all others. Reflect God's goodness to you!

I EXPECT

The work I call on My children to do is not a work of uselessness, but is vital to the raising up the "Family" The Father desires. My work is always on time and timely; therefore the time I call for a task to proceed is just the right time for it to do the most good. My children should appreciate and trust the way I do My business, and always be ready to obey and support My work. I expect this, and I will reward obedience to all that I desire. My work is first and foremost, and I expect My children to see it this way. This note today is a reminder that I am always watching, and always on time. Those who hear Me and obey are the ones I can use and trust.

Let the Holy Spirit guide your thinking. Meditate on the Word of God; saturate your being with His thoughts, His directions, and His promises to you. Let your life and actions flow out of this leading. With God's love as a covering, your thinking will be directed toward others. The love of

God bestowed on you will flow through you and influence the lives of others. However, you must be an open channel. If self becomes a stumbling block the love of God will dissipate. You are a child of God, learning to be like Jesus. Take self out of the picture and release God's goodness to brighten the world around you. This will bring great joy into your life and to your Heavenly Father.

TELL OTHERS

There are many stages, trails, and heights to climb for all of My children; but there is not a one of them that I have not prepared and traveled for you. My dear ones I am your trailblazer; I am your preparer of the Way. If you know all of this already, then tell others, if this is new to you then listen closely. There is no place I have not known about and nowhere you'll ever go that I won't lead, guide, and watch over you. I ask now for you to trust Me and give up all of the self-part of you, because without self I can now take you on trails of blessings and rewards, first for others then for yourself. Your rewards are dependent upon how well you follow the path I lead you on. Yes I will make every day a new trail for you to bless others, and then We will see how well you will be blessed. Come walk each day on the path I lead you.

Rest in Me, and your strength will be renewed. As you wait upon the Lord His thoughts and desires will become a part of your thinking. Act upon the will of the Father as He makes it clear to you, and do not let self get in the way. Strive constantly to draw closer to Me, that We may be One! I have plans for your life, and blessings stored up for you. You are My child, always watched over, protected, and led in the way of righteousness. In praise and worship, and in thanksgiving, allow yourself to be with Me, because We must work together. The things you do without Me are not important in your Spiritual growth, but together much can be accomplished. Open your heart and soul to My directions in your life, and My joy will flood your being.

HEAVENLY PLACE

There are very few times in a man's life that can make him change from what his heart desires into what it should be. What should each man

"Be"? Only what the Father has set for him to be! How many men are brought to that place of perfection? Very, very few, why would that be? God's plan for each man becomes contaminated by earth's environment and man's "self" desires. Self will bring man to nothing; release of self to seek and follow Jesus will draw man into his heavenly place. Man's struggle comes to victory when he gives up "doing it myself" and he lets go and lets God have His will and way. No man can bring himself to perfection, but every man can become perfect in Christ through the Holy Spirit's work. The Father has a plan that draws all men who release self and draws Jesus close. Jesus is the pattern, Jesus is the example, and Jesus is the perfection that all men may claim. Come dear ones draw closer through receiving truth through the Holy Spirit.

When Jesus went home to be with God your Heavenly Father, He sent Me, the Holy Spirit, to earth to abide with you the children of God. As you choose Jesus to be your Lord and Savior I can come and dwell within you to be that teacher, comforter and helper. Your Father did not want you to be alone and without power, I am your seal of salvation. However, you still have free will to call upon Me or to be led by self. There is no Spiritual growth unless I am involved. Being self-led can lead to death. Remember "Those who are led by the Spirit of God, they are the sons of God." My children, release the power and guidance I have for you into your lives. Let the love, peace and joy from God fill your soul. These blessings are awaiting you. Call on Me; listen for My voice, and with Me you shall over-come. Be a part of God's power released in the world.

LIKE JESUS

There isn't any other way for My children to win the race of life, "they must be like Jesus." I have made every provision and prepaid and prepared the way for "whomsoever will." This choice is before each child of Mine daily whether they are aware of it or whether they ignore it, I hold them responsible. My hand extended does not hold back, but is ever ready to save. If only My dear ones would pay a higher price by telling the lost ones all that I've done, and all that I will do, We could save many more than are now coming into the kingdom. Salvation has been paid for but the lost don't know unless someone tells them, how long and how many times do I have to ask you dear ones, "Save the Lost ones," and I will bring them such blessings and rewards that the earth can't contain them. Won't you join the ones that I hold dearest for their sacrifice of love.

The time is now to draw closer to your heavenly Father. This is a time of action, of power, and of fulfillment. The Father is bringing to a close this era of Spiritual growth for His children on earth. It is a time of gathering all His children together, a time of special power and grace, for all who are chosen. Rise up in love and help in the gathering. Let all around you see the light of Jesus in you. Walk in His righteousness, in peace and joy, that others may know Jesus as their Lord and Savior.

STILLNESS AND PEACE

How will I be able to bless, lead, and guide My children when they have such freedom of free will? Only as they release to Me their time daily. This is a real and wonderful thing because of its great potential to bless each child of Mine, but more much more, if each child is truly releasing self and allowing Our Holy Spirit to lead. The work of the Father through his children is where real growth, rewards, and blessings will come. God's work fits into His overall way for drawing all of His Family into His Oneness, that is the goal, the forever walk and way, which every child of God has before him. To draw closer to the Father each day is the walk the Holy Spirit has for each child, therefore your attention should be on what the Holy Spirit has for you to do. You only find this out by seeking him early each morning in stillness and peace.

Being in the center of My love is a place of peace, joy, and protection. Claim this place for you and your family. See everyone with God's hand on him or her, and God's love enfolding each one. God is a family loving God, full of compassion and mercy. Your desire for the well being of family is His desire. Release your loved ones in the care of the heavenly Father. He will guide them through life's trials and tribulations just trust the Lord for He is able. Believe in His word and live the abundant life He has prepared for you and your family.

BE RENEWED

Let a newness come upon you, I give newness and renewing to whomsoever I please. Speak this change, say; "I receive a newness and a renewing in My body right now in Jesus' name." All My children have a walk to walk and a plan from Me to unfold. It is to those who listen and do that I can give new blessings as I please. It pleases Me to bring blessings and rewards to My obedient children. So I say "Be renewed and restored each one who is a doer and seeker of My purpose and plan for him. There is peace and comfort from Me in every trial and testing that I bring. This is found in praise and thanksgiving in and for all things. When this lesson is learned and practiced, real growth occurs, so let praise and thanksgiving ring out in all your walks with Me.

I, the Holy Spirit, am the voice of God in your life, Jesus is your Savior and advocate with the Father, and God Almighty is your Heavenly Father. We are One, all knowing, all power, and all love. Receive all We have for you. Be aware of Our presence in your life, and call on Us. Expect the blessings stored up for you, and walk according to God's will for you. Trust and obey; trust in the promises given you, obey the will of the Father to "Love God with all your heart and your neighbor as yourself." In these two commandments all the ways of the Lord are covered. Draw close daily to your loving Father. Know His will for you and walk in it. He will make a way for you, one with His love, joy, and peace.

THE TOUCHSTONE

When all of this generation of My children see My plan made clear, then I can bring a completion to this age. This time is right before you, and My plan should begin to wind up to its great conclusion. My loved ones should know Me, not just in My truth and in My way, but know Me in My LOVE. No entry will open up until My LOVE becomes the TOUCH-STONE of each ones heart. My dear ones, who listen and are led by My Holy Spirit, this time is "NOW" the flow of My LOVE must become apparent in your lives "NOW" so LOVE can complete My work. Only true LOVE, My LOVE, can set the stage for My return in the air and the great gathering there. Remember the song "LOVE LIFTED ME," here's the truth of that verse made known, for truly it will be only "BY MY LOVE" that My first great catching away takes place!

In Jesus all things have been accomplished, and through Jesus a way was made for you to be saved, to go boldly to the throne of the Father. He made it possible for the children of God to walk in His LOVE, His strength and His peace. He exchanged His bodily presence here on earth for the Holy Spirit, the Comforter, to dwell with man. He did not leave man alone but sent the power of God, as the Holy Spirit, to indwell each one and be their source of LOVE, joy, peace, patience, kindness, goodness, faithfulness, gentleness, and self-control. Rejoice dear one, and have a heart of thanksgiving for this precious gift. Expect and anticipate a close walk with Almighty God by following the lead of the Holy Spirit. It is the way of righteousness to Oneness with Him!

FINAL GATHERING

There is now little time left for My loved ones to become what My plan has set for them. Only the listening, obeying ones will complete this course with knowing. Set your heart to hear My instructions for you, yes each one reading these words is My chosen one, see that I have your full time and attention in these last days. To hear and obey [ALL YOUR WAY EACH DAY IS GIVEN TO YOU BY ME] YOU NEED TO GIVE ALL OF YOUR ATTENTION TO THE THINGS I DESIRE. In this way I can set your feet on your final walk before My catching away. The times before you are final forming times just before your life eternal in your new bodies. What could be more important than the event I've just mentioned? There is no turning back, no ducking out, to miss or ignore what I'm talking about! What have you imagined I've meant when I've talked about My FINAL GATHERING? It is here now and you should know what I'm doing! Wake up, seek your place in the quiet times We have!

A day of rejoicing in the presence of God! What a comfort to know that God is in charge and all things are under His control. He is a God of love so everything He does is for the Spiritual growth of His children. At times there are great trials; perhaps a cleansing is needed, but all things are for the good and growth of the children of God. You are to go through these trials and tribulations walking in righteousness, being an over-comer, and doing the work assigned to you in love and peace. God will see you and your loved ones through. Be led by the Holy Spirit. Trust that all things are working together for good, for God is LOVE!

PERFECTION PERSONIFIED

There is now much to be done to wrap up the children's catching away. Jesus is waiting for a Bride prepared and ready, a Bride that has filled Her place of preparation with perfection and loving care. Oh the joy that awaits the heavens above and the heaven below. Never before and never again a gathering such as this one! Which is a brand new expression of God's loving handiwork manifested as perfection personified. A packaged deal so filled with LOVE'S expansion that the angels above have never see the like of God's LOVE released in beauty, light, and sound displayed for all heaven to view. This will be a wonder to behold of blazing light that all three heavens are stirred and awakened with its brilliant display. Come dear children get caught up with the sweep of joy ad excitement about to be released, and do all the Spirit of God in you leads you to do in preparation!

"I have come that you may have life and that more abundantly," Jesus' words to the church. To have an abundant life you must stay connected to the Lord in prayer, and praise, in worship, and by burying His word in your heart. His presence is about you and is filled with LOVE and compassion for you. His protection is a constant barrier between you and evil, and walking with Him means a life of peace and joy. You should be aware of His presence in your life, walk the path He has prepared for you, listen for His directions, and let His peace fill your soul. Be the child of LOVE He intended you to be! This will bring forth the abundant life Jesus has for you.

NEVER DOUBT

When disaster strikes I am there watching over My loved ones, some are called home because their time is up, others are brought to places of great growth and enduring belief, rising up to display My loving care. Every child of Mine is watched over, no evil occasion ever catches Me unaware.

It is not important to My children what nature does, it is only important what My plan is and how I execute it. Never doubt My place in any natural disaster I am always in charge. Things that occur are but the unfolding of lives lived to prove the things here said. These times are "wrap-up" times. They are times of closing chapters, events of culmination, proving My plan in the long run. Never assume a happening is just a natural event, My hand of control is always at work. My wrath is expressed as evil is released and uncontrolled by My church, My hand is a hand of blessings working in adverse conditions to show My children a better way to go. No person is ever lost by a disaster; I am always overseeing and working My plan of perfection. No child of Mine is ever lost, I am always its Savior in every situation. Rise up to the things your land is experiencing; show forth the loving response I expect from My loved ones. These are times of worth for all who are led by My Spirit. Your prayers are heard, and I am always watching over your loved ones, are they not My loved ones too?

Let today be a step up from yesterday in your Spiritual growth. I would that you go from Glory to Glory in your walk with Me. Allow love to have its way with you this day. This will mean patience, more self-control, meekness and gentleness toward all you meet. This attitude will bring you great joy, and a peace that only God can bring. Walk in a bubble of God's presence with a generous Spirit. As a child of God you are to be a light in this world, the salt of the earth. Do others see your light; has your salt lost its savor? "Let us not be weary in well doing, for in due season we shall reap, if we faint not." These are God's words for us to live by. Do so and live in peace and joy!

CLOSING EVENT

The ongoing life on earth is but a testimony to the plan I have in operation at this time. These times ahead are purposed and planned as a closing event in the ongoing forming of a great family of forever in perfection of all I do. No event is by accident no happening is one of unaware circumstance, all, everything occurring, is but the unfolding of My desire. These times are wake-up times for the to be saved lost ones. My children, called by My name, will be identified by their response to My unfolding will and way. All things will work to fulfill My desires. Do not imagine vain and purposeless events are occurring, only planned unfolding of My pattern of perfection will show forth in the next few months. Draw closer every moment that I give you, My dear ones, do not lay back or relax, these are to be your finest hours.

When your soul feels heavy rest in Him and let His peace lift you up. God has a peace for you that passeth understanding. When you walk in this place all things become possible. These are times to, "Wait upon the Lord and He shall renew your strength." For truly, "The joy of the Lord is your strength." These promises from God's word are for you, child of God. Take them and make them a part of your being. Your Heavenly Father is faithful to perform His word in your life. Trust and obey and life can have a new meaning. Trust His word and obey His commandments to love God and love one another. Experience His presence when you trust in Him.

FINALIZATION

I have many things set to perform in these last days, but none is as important as the forming of a group of "Last Times" warriors. I am building a small army of My best listeners that I can give My words and instructions to. They are to receive daily orders of advance for My Kingdom workers. There will be much released through this channel of workers that will set the stage, just as I desire, for the final completion of My gathering. Yes, there will be an end just ahead to the work of My Bride. Few will understand, but the work will show and all the earth will know that time is up, and clearance will be given by the Father for all of heaven to see and know this great effort has come to finalization. It is no secret that I am "Catching Away" My loved ones. I've broadcast this event over the years by My prophets, and I shall perform that which I have spoken!

When you pray God releases His angels, His ministering Spirits, to act on your behalf. "The effectual fervent prayer of a righteous man availith much," This is God's assurance to you. It is necessary to believe in your heart, to trust God completely when praying and you will receive the answer. Your God is a great God, and a loving Heavenly Father, who wants you to have the desires of your heart. His will for you to grow Spiritually covers all. He wants to lift you up to have a closer walk with Him. You must pray in His will. "Seek ye first the kingdom of God and

His righteousness, and all these things shall be added to you." Pray believing with a heart of thanksgiving to your Abba Father. He hears your prayers!

SO GOOD

To keep this daily walk, staying close to Me, is the only path for the children of My love. My dear ones do not stray or wander off because you never know how close is My "Catching Away." Now is the time to keep your moment-by-moment thoughts on the things I bring you. Now is the time for that "closer walk" to start without end. Now is the closing of this earth's walk for the called ones who have answered and walked with Me daily. There will be no more time like this, these very present hours left to you. Learn to honor the time with Me in the flesh, so you will be comfortable with Me in the Spirit. When change occurs there will be no turning back, ever. These are the great and wonderful last moments of loving decision, setting everlasting life up to its completeness. Never look back on what's behind, because what's ahead is so good!

This is the time to abide in the presence of God. It is a time to show forth the fruit of the Spirit in your life. Let others see the God qualities in your life, the love, patience, self-control and the gentleness that reflects Jesus. Do others around you know you are a Christian? By your actions, your love, and sweet Spirit are you a refection of Jesus? Let the love of Jesus pour forth from your life, be a channel of love to all. His great love is readily available to you, but only as it is passed on to His children. Let His light shine in your life. Walk in His presence, for in His presence is fullness of joy.

FROM NOW ON

Your daily walk should go to a trot and then break into a run, because the end of this age is so near. Keep your eyes on My way, always from now on because We are coming very close to "Take Off" time. Can you believe such a thing is real? Can you trust in Me so much that it passes all human ways of the world? True knowing is a gift I give to all who "Know to whom they belong." Let the world go the world's way, because that is doom and forever lostness, but tell the unsaved how great I am, and how much I gave to save them. This great "Forever Separation" is looming just ahead, be sure you are not leaving anything to tie you to that past! Come dear ones, bringing everyone who you can with you, and We will start afresh in the Father's Kingdom.

Walk in His glorious presence. God is watching over you, available for protection and guidance. You were made to be a child of righteousness, to grow more and more like Jesus His first born Son. You were fashioned to be a part of the Family of God. However you were given free will to choose Almighty God and His righteousness or self and the world. God has shown you the way by His word, the Bible, and by the example of His Son, Jesus. Jesus made the way by His sacrifice to wipe away our sins. So there is no obstacle to our closer walk with Him except self. Can you put down self and be led by the Holy Spirit into a closer walk with your Heavenly Father? It is a walk of love and peace and joy forevermore!

PERFECTION OF UNITY

If every day were actually used to do all that I ask of My children, then would My plan be completed rapidly. But rapidly is not My way, free will so dictates that I stay carefully away from any form of dictatorship. Only those who's free will choice is to follow My desires each day will find completion in Jesus, which should be all My children's goal. So, set your hearts to seek My plan for you, for that is the course required for your victory. All life is found in Jesus, all love is found in Jesus. Every child has the capacity to be like Jesus, to come into the fullness of all He represents. No goal is higher or more worthy. Make Jesus your example and stay on course My dear ones, and I will draw you into the perfection of unity from which all love transpires. Everlasting Oneness is love's plan for you!

God's love is total acceptance. He loves you and accepts you just as you are. He has sent the Holy Spirit to indwell you, so you may grow in righteousness and become more like Jesus. He has blessings for you, and the fruit of the Holy Spirit is waiting to be called upon, and is always available. The first of these blessings is love and through love all the rest will be fulfilled. When you express God's love to others His peace, joy, patience, and gentleness will come forth. Love is truly the key . Let that love of God , so freely given to you, pour out and bless those around you. This fulfills His commandments to you, and draws you ever closer to God. Rejoice in His love!

FULL USEFULNESS

There is no better way for My children to walk than on the path I show them. My path will open up the windows of heaven and bring blessings, first to all those around them, and then unto those who hear, and hearing obey. This message is not new, yet I find very few children who are obedient to what is said. Why is that? Unbelief? Unwillingness to commit? Reluctance to obey what I say? Doubts, fear of results? Why is obeying My will and way so hard? Only one great obstacle lies in the path of each one, SELF! This is a battle I've already won, but having done all I can I wait for My work to bear fruit. It is a simple request, just listen, and hearing do what I say by being led by your Holy Spirit, all effort will be proper and directed in sure ways and paths of victory, but self must take a back seat, DO AS YOU ARE LED DAILY. Start with a simple easy step and I will bring you into your full usefulness.

"All things work together for good to those who love God and are called according to His purpose." This promise from God is for you. If you are walking in His presence and living according to His plan everything in your life will be a blessing. Each circumstance can be a blessing or a learning experience, a correction, or possibly a reward! Be an over-comer and grow from the lessons you are learning each day. Examine self to find what changes are necessary to become more like Jesus Christ. Walk in His love and have a compassionate heart for all of God's children. He will lead you all the way. Walk in His way to victory!

TRUTH REIGNS

When will all My plans come to their perfect conclusion, only when the Father is pleased with and accepts the results. No man knows, but children of God have a "time teller" in their heart. When their heart is true, and they listen to their heart, the true pulse of things will beat out the truth of all things. God, the Father of all, is not a God of secrets but of freedom through truth, as love directs. So God's release of true knowledge is given only as true belief is attained! Love pours out faith, and truth follows as surely as rain falls to the ground. All children stand in God's rain of truth, but their raincoat of unbelief wards off the deep truth. Seek "True Belief" as if it were as precious as air is to breath, then God's truth will flow and fill His reservoir of children with blessings for evermore!

"Thou will keep him in perfect peace, whose mind is stayed on thee." God's word is true. The mind is the battleground and must be brought under control of the Holy Spirit. What is in the mind comes out of the mouth and determines your attitude. Let your thoughts be of peace, goodness, kindness, truth and righteousness, and your words will reflect Jesus. Your attitude then will be of love, peace, and joy. Have a mind filled with praise and worship. "Have the mind of Jesus." This will bring joy to your heart!

MY GREAT DESIRE

There is no other life to live but the life you live through Jesus. Jesus, My Son, dwells in all of My obedient children and they are the continuing source of all that I am doing in the earth and heavens today. Seek, ask for, receive, and enjoy all that I offer through My Holy Spirit, because as you do you give place for OUR life to be accomplished in and through you. Each and every child of God is a vessel of love being nurtured and tended, bringing My Son forth daily to accomplish My planned purposes. No other challenge is so great and wonderful than this pursuit My children are engaged in. I AM, the I AM of all effort in Heaven and earth, and I AM increasing as is MY great desire.

Remember God's great love for the world. Can you let this love flow through you to a dark and unhappy world? You are joint-heirs with Jesus therefore you can be filled with the same kind of love, agape love! Let not self block this channel of love so freely passed on to you by your loving Heavenly Father. The world in its distress needs this special love and peace that comes from knowing God. Be God's light to the world, it is His heart's desire that His children reflect the love of Jesus. Let your world and thoughts reflect His will for you. Let your actions be of mercy, goodness, and kindness, always generous. "Freely, freely you have received, freely give." God is love; you are a child of God, therefore you are a vessel of His love. Reach out to others.

RIGHT AND READY

The moment a lost child of Mine turns to Me for help I am there, what then should a saved child who knows Me be doing? How much more can I do for one who is committed to Me, showing faith by works, and listening and obeying all I say and do? How grand the tasks and great the reach there is when a child of Mine listens, and hearing obeys. Great are the works I still have waiting for those whose hearts are right and ready! In the quiet time of the morning awaken and come to Me, My dear ones. Be still, wait, believe, and listen. I will speak the words of work, and tasks will be given for all to do. Yes, hear from My lips words of work, worth, praise, and directions for this is My call to My loved ones for these times of completion.

I will never leave you nor forsake you. I am closer than you breath for I dwell inside you. You can hear My voice, or not, as you desire. I am the source of many blessings if you will but receive them. Can you let go and be led by Me, the Holy Spirit? For that is to, "Seek ye first the Kingdom of God." You are a joint-heir with Jesus, and have the Glory He has stored up for you. Have the mind of Jesus and walk in His path. I will help you, and you will know the joy and peace of God in your life. Keep your eyes on Jesus and life will be filled with His blessings. Persevere for We are ONE!

FAITH BY DOING

There is little to be left of self if My loved ones heed My voice and set their faces to follow in all I have for them. They will find truth through living, and find faith by doing, and have victory through battles. All this will be as I lead. Only they must never look back. My obedient ones will just look forward to where I point and to where I desire their vision to go. Let everyone who reads, read these things into their heart that they may become heart-led men and women that I am proud of. Only the followers of My hearts desire will find their hearts desires so true. Only I know where I lead, and only My loved ones will see the delights of all I have prepared for them. Keep these words as your "Carrot of Worth" forever, and you shall see, feel, hear, and believe the things I have of unbelievable revelation!

Wait upon the Lord, listen for His voice, follow the directions of the Holy Spirit, and God's will for your life will be fulfilled. Act upon the suggestions God gives to you. Keep the name of Jesus on your lips and in your heart. This name can keep you in God's presence. It will be your covering and protection. This name Jesus, embodies the Spirit of God, the love of God, and imparts it to you. Enjoy being in His presence. Take in the love of the Lord and share it with all others. Walk today expecting God to use you and to bless you. Let joy fill your being because you are a child of God. Have a heart full of thanksgiving and enjoy your walk with the Lord!

A CLOSER WALK

The constant drive of all My children should be a closer walk with Me. It is true when your only desire is to be like Jesus, then your whole body is filled with light, then sin has no hold over you. I have conquered sin and now your task is to believe, receive, and walk in the victory I have attained for you. No child is left out; all have the same opportunity to walk in light as I am in light. All I ask is believing obedience, and then you are set free of Sin, Self, and Satan. My Bride's time is NOW, and I must see this cleansing take place before the final catching away. Drawing closer to Me through the true desire of your heart releases self. Your head [and soul] must submit to your heart's desire, and that desire must be for all I have for you. To be like Jesus is to be filled with light. To act like Jesus is to be obedient to your heart's desire, this walk will release all of self and set you free!

You have an enemy, and that enemy is self. Your self wars against the Spirit. You were given free will to choose, will you choose self and the worldly things, or will you choose the Lord and His Kingdom? To choose God and His righteousness will kill self. But it must be a consistent choice. Remember My words, "Seek ye first the kingdom of God and His righteousness, and all of these things shall be added unto you." God wants to bless you, His child, but if you are self led instead of Spirit led you are blocking the way. Keep your mind on Jesus and His love, and let the Holy Spirit lead you into victory over self!

ENTRY GIFT

The unfolding of My individual plan for each child of Mine is to be done before the "Catching Away." Yes each one will be shown just what is required of them. This is to insure a true blessing for them. The Father has set great works in store for all who will respond. His desires should become your desires so all that then transpires is from Heaven's Vaults of truth. Yes a piece of heaven will come down into each child of God carrying a reward and blessing of eternal worth. This is an entry gift of wonder to bless each child of God. It is as He desires it to be, and truly will have eternal substance of great excellence. All of My children should seek to overcome self, and by this cleansing they are able to receive.

Wait upon the Lord, and rest in the Lord knowing your strength is being renewed. It is through a calm and peaceful Spirit God's power can function. Much in the Spirit world can be accomplished through quiet worship. In the stillness God can speak to you through the Holy Spirit. Let His peace flood your soul. Be lifted up by the power of His Love. God is looking for a receptive heart, a peaceful heart. "Let not your heart be troubled." Let your faith grow knowing your loving Heavenly Father is in charge of all things. His perfect agape love is always your covering.

LOVE FLOWING

There are very few times in each life of My children when I give them a special blessing without their works. My love flows as I desire, and blessings I love to give, just out of My love for each dear one of Mine. In these very last days of this age I have given such blessings. Only to children of obedience and doing do I give. Rewards are for Me a blessing to give; therefore I pleasure Myself when My love releases blessings and rewards. Only My love flowing keeps the earth and heavens in their place, and this keeps Me a blessing to all of My creation. My love flowing is the strength of all I do; this is the lesson here given. Let your love become My love flowing and Our blessings will increase!

"Seek ye first the kingdom of God and His righteousness, and all these things shall be added unto you." You are not to be anxious for anything for Almighty God is your source. Your God shall supply all your needs, so change any fears into faith. Faith that God, who loves you so, knows all about you, and He knows what is best for you, and what is needed in your life for your Spiritual development. God wants the best for you. His love carries protection and supply as well as peace and joy. Persevere in your daily walk with Him and all good things will come to pass in your life. Expect and anticipate the blessings the Lord has planned for you!

KNOWING INTENT

Only by drawing closer to Me in prayer and in true believing can I complete My work in each child of Mine. Our growing together does not happen by quick, quirky miracles, only planned obedience with knowing intent will draw Our walk together into its beautiful conclusion. Our walk is a wonderful togetherness and true submission will result in Our complete and prefect union. Keep this always in mind My dear ones; I will not force your companionship with Me, I will only welcome true desire for it. Come now in full knowledge of Our walk together for there is no other way. Let love of Me replace love of self, then all heaven's wonders will be opened to a foreverness of love.

My plan for you is ongoing. Take one step at a time, learning the lessons of each circumstance set before you. Enter each trial patiently, confident that I am with you, leading and guiding you gently. I will not put upon you more than you can handle with My help. Keep My presence about you for this insures the protection and strength you need. I would that you become a man like Jesus each day. Have the mind of Jesus, the love and compassion, and His patience and peace. All this is possible, as I have planned this way for you. Just walk with Me in love and your Spiritual growth will manifest itself. Remember I am with you always!

THE GOAL SET

When men fail in their every day life they are either broken by it or strengthened by failure. I teach my children in many ways and I will bring failures just as I will bring great success, all because I love them. It is the training and molding of a man into the image of My Son that is the goal I've set for everyone I love. No one can judge My children but Me, no one can lead and guide My children in righteousness but Me. I am the only one with the everlasting goal, and I am the only One, I AM. These are the last days for My Son's Bride, the last days for His church, shouldn't these be the most important days of your life?

Abide always in My love, filled with My peace. It is in this place that you are protected and lifted up. Keep the name Jesus on your lips to guard off the evil in the world. If you will trust in Me and wait upon Me you will go forward in My path, in My plan for your life. My child, you are an over comer, you do have the victory when you stay in My presence. I am your strength and your peace. Go forth each day confident that I am with you. Let My love be your shield and buckler. Trust in the promises I have given you in My word. They are for your daily walk and will see you through. Receive My blessings and walk confidently because you are a child of God.

LOVE EXPANDS

There is a time of "Spurt Growth" in Spiritual matters that I will give every true seeker of My word. No man is ever lost whose heart is for truth. I will draw out everyone who has such a desire in His heart. Truth is a foundation on which love expands. Love is the carrier of all of My desires. So seek truth, find love, and become ONE with Me. Every child born is born to this purpose and few there are who find the love in truth. I seek all who are sincere and all who persist; no one will ever be lost who has these attractions for their goal. Keep your thoughts pure, your actions pure, your walk pure, and see and know daily the blessings I will release. Test Me, try Me by exercising what I say, and you will be one of My blessings!

God is your source of all things. All your needs will be supplied when you are walking and trusting in the Lord. His presence guarantees protection, love, and peace. He truly is a God of abundance. "Seek ye first the kingdom of God and His righteousness." Test the Lord and see that His promise to you, that all things will be added unto you, is true. He is a loving

God, your Creator. He desires that you become more like His Son Jesus, each day. You are a member of the family of God. Walk in this position confident that a loving Father is leading the way.

SELF-LED ONES

There are no lost souls; there are only "Self-led Ones." When you witness to someone believe I am there with you, seeking to save that one from himself. Many are not aware of their own ability to take themselves to death and hell. Pray before you witness, calling on Me to intercede by preparing your way. Only with My help will anyone be saved. Keep this in your mind, and then your compassion will grow for the lost ones and love will prepare a path on least resistance. We are a team only when you make Us one, I am always ready, always waiting, and the field of salvations is always before Us.

Walk in faith, trusting that God is control. He is watching over you and his love is your covering. You have been given a measure of faith, so use what you have and develop it into a mountain of faith. Draw upon the fruit of the Spirit. Release into your life the love, peace, and joy the Father has given you. See others with patience and goodness, and let kindness be your banner, and self-control your goal. The Holy Spirit will help you as you quietly listen for His voice. I am always with you. Remember that and walk in victory!

JUDGMENT

When all men are awakened to truth it will be the time of beginning disaster for all those who never heard truth, or didn't believe it when truth was told to them. Yes all men will know truth; those who believe, receive, and walk in truth have begun an everlasting path of love and victory. Those who hear truth for the last time will be lost forever. Their unbelief or their never caring to seek truth is the cause of their loss. The Great White Throne Judgment will bring the truth of all creation to every lost one. They will be shown truth in all of its beauty and they will know their loss as a beginning of everlasting torment. No man mocks God; all men shall know Him as truth forever. My dear children I hate that coming time of revelation, My heart breaks because of the lost children, won't you seek and save all of those We can right now!

You who know Me have been forgiven and washed clean by the blood of Jesus. Receive and accept this cleansing, and know that God has forgiven and forgotten all your sins. Your Father sees you through Jesus and His love. There is now no condemnation to those who love the Lord. Accept God's word to you and walk in freedom from guilt. Go forth in victory knowing you are a child of God, set free to do God's will. Receive the blessings stored up for you and be a channel of love to others. You can be a beacon of God's light in this dark world for you are in this world but not of it. You belong to the family of God and therefore are sanctified or set aside for the work of the Heavenly Father. Rejoice in the love of God and be filled with joy!

A FAMILY

There is no good thing in any man until he allows Me to send the Holy Spirit within him. This is the plan of a loving Father, who has created the Heavens and the Earth, just for a place of birth and growth for the unfolding of His dream for a family just like His Son! This dream unfolds daily all around you, but are you, aiding and helping in its progress? Or are you even part of it? Have you accepted Jesus then just relaxed believing that has set you in heaven? Wake up dear one if that is so, because you have only begun your journey. My children, called by My name, are required to follow the path I have laid out for them. This is a daily progression never ending! So have you come to some kind of an end on your own? Wake up, seek My voice, and be led by My Spirit, every moment of every day, until I say, "Well done My child."

Every child of God should give praise to Almighty God for He is your loving Father. The Creator of all things is watching over you with love and patience. He sees you as perfected, through the eyes of Jesus. He wants to pour out blessings from heaven upon you, as you turn to Him and walk in the way He has planned for you. God has given you an example to follow in Jesus. He has given you directions for life in His word, the Bible. He sent the Holy Spirit to indwell you and to be a helper and comforter. Oh child of God, turn to your Heavenly Father in praise and worship. He will see you through to victory in your life. Rejoice, for in His presence is fullness of joy!

SIMPLE TRUTHS

All I say is true and truth, but all I ask for is believing. To believe the things I give My children will only fall on willing hearts that listen and believe, then obey and do. Some things I say sound simple but they are not because of the great importance of truth behind them. Simple truths build "Universes". Simple truth creates life, and releases love flowing. Simple things like unbelief stop my simple truths. My simple truths create magnificent, huge, vast heavens of wonders that seeing man can see but not know, feel, or inspect. All this today is but the lifting of the veil, and showing what believing may reveal to My achieving loved ones.

Live in God's presence for in His presence is love, joy and peace. In His presence is the strength and wisdom to do all things. As you walk in His shadow all things are made clear, so you may go forth boldly knowing you are sanctified and being directed by the Holy Spirit. The word says to "Have the mind of Christ." This is possible as you dwell in His presence. He makes all things possible for your Spiritual growth as you constantly recognize Him and look to Him. His presence will cause you to be an over-comer, for your strength is renewed daily. Persevere for God is with you, His Glory and love enables you to think and act always as a child of God. You have been redeemed so rejoice in His mighty presence!

TIME ALONE

There are many things of interest I wish to bring to My children but they are so reluctant to sit and abide with Me. Just sitting and listening can bring forth such wonderful thoughts, ideas, and suggestions. If only I could encourage enough of them to take time alone with Me We could discuss such wonderful new things, ideas, thoughts and suggestions. I have plans of great interest to be explored, and I have purposes of true worth to be accomplished. But how can I bring such things to children who won't take time with Me, to seek a closer walk, to have a closer encounter in all of My plans and ways.

Know you are My child and I am your loving Heavenly Father. I have many blessings waiting for you but you cannot receive them if you are double-minded. Hold fast to the truth that you are joint-heirs with My Son Jesus. Persevere in the daily walk I put before you. I am with you to help you over-come. It is in the little things that Spiritual growth is made. Walk constantly in My love and strength. Dwell in My peace and the way will be made smooth. Keep your eyes on Jesus and His way for you will be made known. Reach out for and hold fast the victory, which is yours through Jesus Christ.

ALL I SAY

The teaching I give to My loved ones is a requirement of Mine I give to all of them. I require their attention and their efforts to hear and obey all I say, this is not because it will aid, support, supply, or enable Me in any way. No I require that they listen, absorb, react, and do the things I say because it will be to all of their benefits, not just now in the earth but it will be building a foundation for their eternal place with Us. What I give them now is an opportunity to participate in their own Spirit placement. I have a place prepared for each and every one of My loved ones and they should wake up to My great plans and efforts now, for this is the winding up to My great effort, "The Catching Away."

Abide in His presence. Let self melt away in the awareness of Almighty God. The way to reduce the influence of self is to fill your soul and being with God and His love. His perfect love will diminish self and loose the beautiful fruit of the Spirit in your life. God's blessings are so much greater than anything man can imagine. They are ready and available for His children, for those that call on Him. Turn your eyes upon Jesus, and praise and worship your Lord and Savior that He may lead you into a closer walk with the Heavenly Father. This is the way to a victorious life in the lord. Rejoice as the blessings cover you, always, now, and eternally.

LOVE'S HEAVEN

There is time and times but time is only a passing. Only what We accomplish together makes your time fruitful. Never believe I am not with you, never believe I am not leading and guiding, never believe your life is wasting, never believe I will not raise you up. Only believe I am truth, I am with you always, and I am taking you on your journey to LOVE'S HEAVEN. Only believe you are an eternal child of Father God, only believe you are important to Us, and We love you. Only believe you have purpose and a place forever with Us. As you believe in truth, truth proves out. Your unbelief unravels truth and spoils truth's way. Oh My children learn about time, truths, and believing, and understand all of My ways for you by listening to My voice in your heart. Open your hearts to the wonders of "Believing" in all I Say!

Enjoy your walk with the Lord, and be thankful for the many blessings you have received. Open your eyes to the beauty of the world, and the beauty in others around you. Rejoice that a loving God who truly is your Father, your Heavenly Father, has chosen you. He created you to be a part of His family and He has plans for your life and your eternity. Walk each day in joy because there is a wonderful purpose for your life. Go forth expecting to be led by the Holy Spirit. Use every circumstance as a growing experience of the Spirit. Hold tight to your Lord's hand, and He will make a way for you, live in His presence and your joy will be full.

CAREFULLY READ

When all My efforts to gather My children are over, there will be no recourse for anyone who has missed the opportunity to be with Me forever in Heaven. My way is set, My plan has no variations, My purposes will be fulfilled, and My Family will be complete. Carefully read this note today! Can you think of someone who doesn't know Me! Then you are here-by commissioned to claim and call to Me for their salvation. I have come to the time of last gathering for the Bride of Christ and this is a wind-up call. If you know Me as "Abba Father," then We are ONE in this gathering and "ONE" shall be all who are included in this wrap-up time. By your prayers and witnessing We will make great this reward for JESUS!

Look up My child, for your strength cometh from the Lord on High! God is constantly supplying all you need to do any task He has put before you. He is your source of all things. Call on Him constantly for peace, strength, patience, and wisdom, and if you walk in His presence, His love, and protection will cover you. His Glory is available to all, but preoccupation with self or the world will block it out. I call you to break through this barrier of self and walk in His love! Keep the name of Jesus on your lips, and restore that circle of God's love and Glory about you. Walk in the way of My commandments and I will lead you to victory. You are My chosen one, trust in Me!

OUR WORK

Very few of My children will listen for Me all day long, why is that? First I'm not requiring such a thing, I expect each one to be on their own ready to be led by Me. My leading will bring them to the place I require, and then they are to be moved to obedience to My prompting. We are a team and a team depends on reliability. My children are to be reliable as I am reliable. Our work is Our walk together, together means joint action, joint responsibility with shared rewards. When My children know Me, then they are part of all of Our actions because of closeness and love. Let all day, each day, become Our shared love walk, and Our togetherness will grow.

"Greater is He that is in you than he that is in the world." Therefore fear not, you have the power of the Holy Spirit indwelling you. This is the same power that raised Jesus from the dead. It is the gift to you from Almighty God, Creator of all things. He is your comforter and helper always ready to release the blessings He has for you, blessings of faith, love, peace, patience, joy, and whatever you need for your Spiritual growth. Call upon Him and bring forth a new power in your life. Live a full life, a life of love that the Father has planned for you!

SPECIAL CALLING

There is a time that I call My loved ones to come into a closer walk with Me. This is a time of special calling, a step into the higher life which I give to those children who are moving with My Spirit and Me. Listen all you who hunger and thirst for more of Me, and are willing to commit to that walk. The blessings I give are for release to the children around you, lost and saved ones. The Blessings I give are everlasting fruit to be savored always. The blessings I give are without peer or comparison. Seek this closer walk as you would diamonds and pearls, ask and I will answer, call out your desire and I will hear. Let Our intimate times flow freely. Let My harvest begin!

Hear the voice of the Lord and you will be shown the way. Jesus said, "I am the way, the truth, and the life." So you should make your way His way. He is the truth, so find truth in Him. Nothing else can be truth outside of Him. Because He is the life, let His perfect life live through you. It will make you complete, blessed, and filled with joy. Have the mind of Christ. Put a guard over your thoughts and the words of your mouth. You are in control so be aware of negative thoughts and cast them out in favor of "God" thoughts. Truly, "Let the words of my mouth and the meditations of my heart be acceptable in thy sight, Oh Lord my strength and my redeemer." As a man thinketh, so is he. Be God's child in thoughts, words, and deeds, and He will fill you with joy!

MAKE MY DAY

There are many ways for Me to lead My children into a closer walk, but the one I look for and prefer is when they, on their own, rush to walk and talk with Me each day. When I find desire for Me so compelling that My loved ones look for, seek, and draw close to Me every chance they get, then I am blessed! My dear ones make your way My way every day, and the whole world will take on a new meaning. Our way will take every wrong and make them right. Our way will bring joy, peace, and well being to all about Us. Release My love in your daily walk and see the blessings I release all about you. Come try and test these words today, let your faith be displayed and My day made!

God is your source of all things. Do not look elsewhere. He is providing your health, your strength, and your wisdom and financial blessings. His plan for you is unfolding, and you are growing Spiritually as you live your life through Him. Let go of self and selfish desires and allow God to direct the way. His way is blessed and one of developing the Spirit. You have a measure of faith but you must grow into a mature Christian with abundant faith. You have love, but His agape love is available bringing great Glory and power into your life. Let His peace flood your soul to develop patience and gentleness. "My God can supply all your needs." Walk ever closer with Him.

I CALL

There are many meanings to My call on a man. I call because he needs My help, I call because My love is needed in his life, I call for his benefit daily, I call because My plan has a place for him to fulfill, but above all I call him just because I love him and want him to love Me and all of My ways. My dear ones My call is all, all you will ever need. My call has eternal life's most pleasant blessings. My call has a beginning but no ending. My call is not loud or audible, but a still silent voice in your heart. Can you dear ones hear My call? We have been about you calling for a long time, isn't it time you should answer? If you stir yourself, and spend time with Me, I can take you to a deeper call!

"Thy word is a lamp unto my feet, and a light unto my path." Let God's word direct your path and you will walk in His light. As God is love, so is He light. In Him there is no darkness. When the darkness of the world threatens to engulf you look to your Savior for the light. It is available to you because you are a child of the living God. Let His light permeate your being and reflect it to others. In the light is discernment and Godly wisdom. In His light is peace of mind and clear thinking. Keep your eyes on Jesus and you will walk in His light, and in perseverance you will develop the mind of Christ. In His light is joy forevermore.

CONTEMPLATE

In every man's heart is a place for Me to abide, and when We are thus together it is a match made in Heaven that's given for eternity. My dear ones take time to contemplate just what has been said. I, the Creator of All, have claimed to abide forever in Man! How can that be, only because I desired to so live through each dear one of My children. Never doubt the fact that I have just claimed, because what I decree is so! We are ONE FOREVER! Why am I making this statement here and now, only because My children are so slow to wake up to the stupendous wonder of all this. My express wish is to have a loving family that I may enjoy always, and this gesture is so thought provoking no one else can grasp the true significance of this blessing of true love expanding. Never- the- less it is so!

My children remember that you are the temple of the Holy Spirit. The Holy Spirit is all of God given to man, God's love, peace, joy, wisdom, and His faith, patience, gentleness, goodness and self-control. You are to release these blessings into your life to be effective for the Lord. Be open and receptive to the Holy Spirit. Only through His directions can you grow Spiritually. He is truly your comforter and helper, a gift from the Father, given when you accepted His Son, Jesus, as your Lord and Savior. Do not ignore this precious gift. It will change your life into a glorious adventure as the Holy Spirit leads you.

CLEAR PATH

The meaning of words, wherever they come from, should be left up to Me. Many times men say things to you that doesn't seem right but their intent is misconstrued, don't be upset with men, ask Me for truth. I know the intent of hearts and I will help keep you on the straight and clear path. My dear ones keep Me in all you do, all you hear, and all you desire. Why should I ask such a thing now? My dear ones how many times must I tell you your time in this time is very short, and only by drawing closer to Me "all of the time you have left" will I be able to draw you into a better place. Come closer while We can improve Our Oneness. Come closer for Jesus' sake!

God operates in the now. He would have you live in the present. The past is behind you, leave it, forget it and press on. Today is the day of the Lord. He has given you 24 hours, how will you use them? Walk in peace this day. Rest in the Lord and truly your strength will be renewed. Enjoy the beauties of the world about you and see the good in everyone you meet. The Lord is with you to help you overcome all trials and tribulations that come your way. "Trust in the Lord with all your heart, and He shall direct your path." Let this be the promise in your heart, and each day will be filled with joy.

VALUE OF TIME

When time seems to drag on, are you really paying attention to the unsearchable value of time? Time is a factor of living that I give freely for My children to have the life experience that I'm believing will bring them to Me. I have life eternal, which is when TIME is OVER! [There will be no calculation of hours and such.] No child of Mine knows yet about My eternity. In human minds the concept is unfathomable in its true reality. How can man concept "Always" as an existence? How can endless be explained, what could possibly relate to it? Even go back to ""Always has been!" Please give clear understanding of that! Does "Always has been" go back in the past as far as endless time ahead can go? Dear ones give proper perspective to the time you have left!

The Glory of the Lord is round about you. In this Glory is God's love and His peace. Take of it and walk in it daily. The Lord is supplying all your needs so be at peace. Let go and let God help you with the decisions necessary, and He will give you the Godly wisdom to walk in His path. Go forth boldly, confident that He is with you. Anticipate and expect the blessings that God wants to bring into your life. Praise and worship your Heavenly Father at all times and the problems of the world will fade away.

EARTH TIME

There are a few of My children that will spend their time with Me enough so We can do a work together. These ones are useful now and they are the ones I find will become more useful in any later endeavor I may desire. You must understand the purpose for which I use this earth time. It is not just to give men an opportunity to be saved from death and hell but for man to be lifted up and up until they truly become My Sons and daughters forever! Your time on earth in the flesh of man is but a "Way Stop" on your growth to becoming like Jesus. It is most important that you bring yourself completely to Me and release the "Self" that I gave to get you there. Your life with Me on earth is the most important place and time you will "ever" have. Wake up to the requirement I've just put before you, and Wake up and answer My call, be there "All of the time you have left!"

My child be aware of the Spirit World around you. Listen for the voice of the Holy Spirit within. He is eager to lead and guide you, to teach and to comfort. He is all truth. When you walk in the way of the Spirit there are no mistakes. Each encounter is arranged and watched over by Me. All is planned for your Spiritual growth or for the benefit of those around you. At this time I am pouring out My love in the world. Will you share yours with those who do not know Me? As a member of My family, will you spread My agape love to My lost sheep? They must have an opportunity to know Me before it is too late. I am eager for the gathering of My loved ones but no one must be left out. Show forth My Glory, that all will know of My love and choose Jesus as their Savior. Trust in Me I will show the way.

LOVE PAVES THE WAY

When I make a call upon a child of Mine it is not because I need him, it is because I love him. My call is a call of love. How many have thought otherwise? I call those I know I can trust, and I expect their work to be just what I require. In My family love paves the way, therefore all the ways of My called ones become ways of love. My children hear and answer My call, they know what it is, and there isn't any confusion and or doubt. Now dear ones do I call every child of Mine? Of course I do, I have a place and a plan for each one because each one is important to Me. If this call is clear then are you hearing and answering My call to you? Do you listen for Me, and then to Me? Are We in close touch and communication? Why not? Come dear ones seek My call. Lets' have a closer walk!

Focus on God and His love and not on the problems in your life. Focus also on the word and His promises to you. "My God shall supply all my needs according to His riches in Glory, through Jesus Christ." Lean on and trust in the Lord to see you through. Remember He has sent His ministering spirits, angels, to watch over you. You are His creation, His child, and He has great plans for your life here on earth and for your eternal life. Let His love strengthen you and guide you along the path He would have you walk. Keep your eyes upon Jesus and you will be lifted up to heavenly places.

WHERE ARE YOU GOING?

In a man's life is time for all that I call him to be and do. It is not his call upon his heart that should drive him, but My call upon his heart in which he should find great pleasure and reward. It is the same for all men, sometime they should all stop and consider who are they, where did they come from, and where are they to go? No questions are more important to man than to find the true answer to those questions. Churches, Mosques, and places of worship made for man's ideas will never fulfill the desire in men's hearts. Only truth will prevail. I am truth and I soon must go into a different time than this, but you children should know and make full use of these last wonderful times you are now living in. Tell the lost about Our love and show it to them, leave none behind!

The sun, moon, and stars reflect God's love for you. All the beauty of the earth was created for God's family. You are a member of the family of God, covered by His love, protected and favored. His command is to love God and to love others. By obeying this commandment you will walk the straight and narrow path into God's kingdom. Enter into every situation covered by God's love and His wisdom will guide you. Walk uprightly knowing you are loved and that your Heavenly Father is always with you. Give up self and selfish thoughts as you seek to do the will of your Father. He will show the way. Persevere in God's love knowing all is well.

NEXT PLACE

In My arms rests My entire dear ones that I called to Me. I lose none and all My children come to Me. This is the hope and the reality of My love. When those times and lives on earth are over, then I lift My loved ones to their next place of abiding, to be with Me in My light and enlightenment. To grow in knowledge of Me is life eternal and I have many phases and times still to be walked through and all of My loved ones live the same path of victory. Step by step, glory to glory just as I have said. My children are all different but the same to Me; My walk with each one has a great variety of adventures and paths of wondering and learning. In this everyone grows into just what the Father's heart has desired. Keep this picture of your way open always to the new and different because the Father is never boring.

All is well, and God does all things rightly, and He is in charge. His plan is perfect for you, walk each day being led by the Holy Spirit. Each incident, each trial, every happening, can be a lesson learned, another step upward in your Spiritual growth. Persevere in God's strength, His peace, and His wisdom. Receive the blessings He has for you. Walk uprightly according to the word of the Lord. Live in peace and joy as you anticipate and long for your blessed eternity with the Heavenly Father. Walk in love and you "will receive that crown of life that God has promised to those who love Him."

PRIMARY GOAL

In drawing men closer to Me, it is the job of My children to be first in this effort. Only loving Me is first, and then loving My children should be next in their daily work and thrust of desire. Seek to fulfill this, My desire, and all of your life's work will be successful. This is the primary goal each one should have, to love Me and love My children. When this is a heart's desire, then I can freely support, lead, and guide with great enthusiasm the obedient ones. When a life is given to this purpose I should find a child of Mine so caught up in love for others that it becomes a driving force of works. Our way on earth is the way of obedient love in all works of the flesh, have this as your goal and We will become, very soon, ONE!

This is a time of learning. You have been given free will to choose God or to choose self and the world. Having made your choice, to follow Almighty God, this earth time is preparing you for an eternity with the Father. Immerge yourself in the word, learn and practice My commandments and promises to you. Seek My face and listen for the guidance of the Holy Spirit. Walk gently in love, enjoy and take in My presence, which is all about you. See others through the eyes of Jesus, seeing only the good in them. Walk on with no condemnation, receiving the forgiveness God has granted you. You have been redeemed, and set free, to live in love and to enjoy a close walk with your Heavenly Father. Rejoice My child, soon We will be together.

REALLY LISTEN

Into every man's life I bring just the things that would lift him up and draw him closer to Me, but it is the things he brings into his life that tear him down. How long will you, My children, be like other men? There is just time left for all of you now to turn to Me in repentance, and seek the walk I would give you. There is just enough time left for those who will obey and finish the walk they should take to bring them into the place I desire they should be. Hear now this word all you who know Me, and turn around from your ways and walk the way I would lead you. Do not be fooled about what is here said, all will prove out to truth. Do you really listen to truth?

In the quiet time of the morning sit in silence and focus on Me. Seek My face and dwell on My word and promises to you. Bask in the sunshine of My presence. Take into your being My agape love that is being poured out upon My children. My presence will make the difference in your life, darkness must flee and My light covers all. In My light is health and healing and the peace that passes understanding. When searching for directions for your life in My presence all things become clear and answers come forth. Wait upon Me and truly you shall be renewed. We are drawing closer, rejoice, for the goal is near.

DAILY WALK

There are times of trouble and times of joy, but the times that will count in eternity are only the times you walked with Me. Your awareness of My presence is the sign of pending victory. Keep your daily time the time We are One and all your walk will be as planned. I have set a course for each child of Mine and few are there who follow perfectly. What I look for is "Desire" in the hearts of My children. What is your constant desire? Self-pleasing or God pleasing, this is basic in daily victory. You are the only judge of your obedience, I do not judge you, but I only seek to encourage you in your daily walk. Keep this word close to your heart and seek the obedience of compliance.

God is in charge, let Him direct your life, and you will have joy. "Trust in the Lord with all your heart. Lean not on your own understanding. In all your ways acknowledge Him and He will direct your paths." God's word for His children gives direction and encouragement. He will direct your path if you seek His face. His way is always best, and the rewards are awaiting you. There is joy in a walk with Him, one with peace and happiness. God would that you have an abundant life; you should live it as a faithful child of God.

INWARD BELIEVING

There are many ways for My children to find Me, but the best way is to have a true desire believing I am, and that I will reward those who find Me. There is an authentic inward believing that I release to those who's hearts are right, to those who believe in My heavens and My earth. Have I not said I give the heavens and earth that men shall know Me? My dear ones think it not a strange thing when someone so easily and quickly accepts Me when you give them the chance. I prepare hearts in many ways and I am always at work. If you will just open up to My lost ones I will surprise you with many hearts already prepared. Be bold My dear ones in seeking the lost for now is the time for a great harvest!

Keep your eyes off of self, and things of the world, and on Jesus Christ. Have a seeking heart learning of His love and His promises to you. Study His commandments and make them a part of your life. Seek knowledge of God and His plan for His children, and His plan for your life. In all activities make God the corner stone. Think, "What would Jesus do in this situation?" He is your example and the Bible is your manual for life. Take joy in knowing Him, in pleasing Him, for His love is ever a part of you. Have a heart of thanksgiving and walk in His presence every day.

GREAT PLANS

All I desire to give My children is a closer walk with Me through Our Holy Spirit. When will all My children come to know the blessings bound up in that One who dwells in them? Come My dear ones no longer hold back or doubt in your hearts that I have great plans for you, Yes, YOU who are now reading these words are the precious ones that I seek daily.

Take this note as a personnel invitation if you never have moved in obedience to My words. Move now in clear acceptance of the things here said I am again calling out to you to draw close to US each morning and wait upon Our words to you. Only by you receiving Our directions to you can you ever learn to walk the walk of Our plan for you. Listen in your Spiritself and know the truth I have to share just with you each day.

Remember you were created in love and with a purpose. The World, even the Universe, was created for you, God's child, to have a place to grow Spiritually, and prepare yourself to be one with God in eternity. God created you for a purpose. There is a reason you are here. You are to fit rightly in God's Family, the Bride of Christ. Almighty God had a plan for your life when you were created. By searching in his word, by seeking His face and His presence in your life, you will learn His special purpose for you. As you walk through life daily remember, "It is all about God" not self, and your goal is to please God Not Self. Do you respond, to His abundant love being poured out on You, with love and joy and a desire to please Him, your Heavenly Father? He takes great pleasure in everything you do, in all you are, live today for Him!

MY THINGS

There are many openings made for My children to draw closer to Me daily if they will only grasp them. I never leave My dear ones, and I never cease trying to draw them into a closer walk. My voice is a still small voice and it is seldom listened to because self and ego are constant roadblocks to their Spiritual growth. My school of the Spirit is always open but so few are there who enter into it. Rise early, listen well, and come into the new growth I daily have for you. Read your Bible, talk with Me, and enter into Our walk daily. Why should I cry out like this? I draw those whose desire is for My things. Do you really have a desire for a closer walk daily? Don't dodge this question any longer; your time is just about over!

Think in terms of eternity, of forever. This time on earth is a time of preparation. You are being prepared for your eternity with Jesus Christ and Almighty God. Your Heavenly Father will lead and guide you; He will show you the way. After accepting Jesus as your Lord and Savior you must walk in the way God has planned for you. You were created with a purpose for your life. If you live and walk in that purpose your life will be complete and fulfilled. This is the way to have joy and peace as you learn and overcome the lessons here on earth. Do not be distracted by worldly things. Find God's purpose for your life and pursue it with all your heart. Persevere, you are not alone, I am with you and My love covers you always!

WALKING THE WALK

Every day I hide a blessing for each of My children. It is received at their compliance with My will for them at that time. This is a game I play to keep everyone happy in My work. Not many are able to enjoy to the fullest this loving action of Mine because of their slow obedience and lack of communication with Me. My blessed ones are those who listen, hear, and obey. They are the ones walking the walk I lead them on. Only by daily conferring with Me will all of My children find the true walk I have prepared for them. Seek this as if it were gold and silver because its worth will far exceed mere coin of men. Each day can be a "growing closer" walks when obedience through love is flowing. Come dear ones and check out what is here revealed!

Your life should be lived to give Glory to God. You can give Glory to God by being what He created you to be, by fulfilling His purpose for you here on earth. You are to recognize that He is Almighty God, your Heavenly Father, with a heart of thanksgiving and praise. Love your fellow man for God loves him too. God is love and He loves you now and forever. Your Father is supplying all your needs and desires, as you love the life you were created for. Be the child of God that gives Him Glory as you show forth the love, peace, and joy of the Lord. Walk in His presence and be led by His great love.

FOREVER ONENESS

When all time has spent itself and the truth of Jesus has been shown to the entire world, then will I lift every barrier, every obstacle, and every hindrance, then My full wonder of love shall flow like a river and all the heavens and earth shall rejoice and be glad. The Heavenly Family of God will be fully known and the beauty of My love shall be exposed for all shall be My family forever. Sorrow, shame, upset, and turmoil no longer will have exposure, for love washes out all evil and loves completion of beauty and happiness will fill the Universe. My heavens will sing with happiness and nothing will be out of place, but all will know God's plan on Love Expanding. All God's children will no longer be called children, but all will walk with the newness of Forever Oneness as equal members of the Father's Family.

My child spend time with Me today, and worship your Heavenly Father in all ways. Worship in song and praise, and prayer, but also worship in all your actions. Worship is pleasing God, as a little child seeks to please his father. Live in an attitude of worship. You Heavenly Father is pleased with you; He loves you with an overwhelming love, an Agape love. He sees you through Me, Jesus. He will help you grow Spiritually as you reach out to Him. He has given you the Holy Spirit to lead and guide you, to be your comforter and helper. Worship God today in a new way. Seek to please the One who is your source of all things. Let love lead the way.

HIS DESIRE

There are many ways for man to see God, but no man will ever see Me on his own. Only the ones I draw unto Myself will ever know the God of All. God is in, through, above, and about all of His creation, all of the time, and most of the works of His hand never know Him. It is only important that the children of His desire do so. The revelation to man of their Creator is a God timed release of recognition. This only comes about when man's heart is a "Truth Seeking One". The revelation of who God is can never be seen all at once. The slow unveiling of "Truth's Wonder" comes only as mutual acceptance grows in the heart of man, then into his soul. Until Spirit and Soul can see together the true hand of their Creator's works man can only seek truth in wondering. Call out dear ones and be open to all your loving Heavenly Father has for you, because your last time to do so freely is fast diminishing.

Trust in the Lord and obey His commandments. Because He created you in love, because God is love, everything He commands you to do is for your good. He sees the overall picture of your life and knows what is needed for your Spiritual growth. God is constantly attempting to draw you closer to Him. He does this through the trials and tribulations in your life and by pouring out an abundance of blessings daily. See and be aware of what God is doing in your life. Are you cooperating with Him or doing your own thing? Is self in control or is your Heavenly Father leading you? The word says, "Be led by the Holy Spirit is to be a son of God." My child let Me lead you in this path of righteousness and your joy will be full.

NEVER DOUBT

I direct these words to you each day because I desire My words to flow on to all of My children. It is only My desire being fulfilled so never doubt or relax into unbelief. Continue in this that is given and you will see and know all of the things I say are true. I have not set this task before others like I have with you so keep close and keep on as you are. It is through this flow of My words that I pour truth out in an acceptable manner for My children to grasp. Not all will accept or believe, that is My problem not yours. Take each day just as you have been, because so far this is all I've required. Just know what I say here is all that needs to be said.

Surrender your life to God and have freedom and power in your life. God is able to release you from fear and worry as you let go and let God. Trust in your heavenly Father for He loves you, and wants the best for you. His plan will bring peace of mind and joy surpassing anything you can imagine. He created you with a purpose. When you are fulfilling that purpose His peace will engulf you and you will know His joy. Being submissive to God will bring forth a new and improved you, the special person God intended you to be. His love will transform you and make you whole. Today let God fill your life with new meaning. Walk in His Love.

WILL THEY LISTEN?

There are so many things My children need to know, and how to draw them into a listening mood is the first step to be accomplished. Will they listen if I promise to speak and teach them each morning? Some will, some may, and most won't take the time, isn't that sad? How must I teach them when they won't sit still and listen? My teachers must move on their hearts as I lead, and between Us We can draw many into a growing place. It is with this purpose I give instructions each morning for you to record that there will be left a written record of My efforts on their behalf. Today, as is every day, this message is given seeking to draw the unworthy into their place of great worth. They are unworthy because of their reluctance; they are made worthy by their attention. Pay attention all My children who I draw into this circle of love, Our times of joy are but beginning.

Meditate on God and His goodness all day long. "Let the mind of Christ Jesus be in you." Be aware of the many blessings He has showered upon you. Talk things over with God, and allow Him to be a part of your life. "In all your ways acknowledge Him and He shall direct your paths." He is always with you and He has all the answers, answers for your Spiritual growth. As you meditate on Him, or focus on Him, listen for the directions He has for you. His way is always best. He sees the whole picture, knows the beginning and the end, and He has great love for you, His child. Walk in the path He has prepared for you and you shall have a Glorious life in Christ.

ANSWER READILY

Only My chosen ones are fulfilling My plan. It is through their efforts, led by My Spirit, that all proceeds in perfect timing and order. There are no obstacles to My plan that are not overcome. Our work is always on time and perfect in all results. Why bring this to your attention now? Because there are always wrong influences trying to derail and make of no purpose the things My children do. Never be turned aside from My purposes shown to you, always turn to Me for help. Call out and ask "Jesus help me" and I will hear and answer readily. Never continue in wrong ways and wrong directions, always recognize the errors and call out for help. This is a reminder of the dangers that lurk to your detriment. Do not be misled or mistaken!

Can you see God as a best friend? One who desires your love and affection? He wants to have honest open communication with you, His child. He already knows your every word and thought. He understands your feelings, good and bad, so be honest with Him. Tell Him of your doubts

and questions, and then listen for His answers, His solution to your problems. In His great love for you He wants to give you the desires of your
heart, but He must allow you your free will. You must freely seek Him,
desire His way for your life and be aware of His presence. Remember His
agape love and His ever-abiding presence and you will walk in His plan
for greater joy and peace.

FAITH TO DRAW

The victory for My loved ones lies in their ability to receive and believe
all the things I tell them. I have given them good health; prosperity, long
life, happiness, and well being, but they must also take up this word for
them and by faith walk in all I've done. I said "It is Finished" that meant
all I could do for My loved ones was already accomplished in the Spirit
realm. What is needed is faith to draw all the blessings into the physical
realm. This is the challenge and work that is set before each one. All are
in the same position of working out their own way with Me. My hand is
extended daily toward all, and nothing will be held back when belief
equals desire. Set this note before you daily and by your believing actions
receive all I've prepared for you.

Let the word of God dwell within you. It creates and maintains health in
your body. The power of the Holy Spirit permeates your whole being and
it is activated by the words of your mouth. Because you have been given
free will you are in charge. Tell your body what the word of God says
about health and it will respond. Believe what God has given you in His
word, the promises of life in abundance. Your body is truly the temple of
the Holy Spirit. Allow and direct that body to have the health God intended for you in His word. There is power in the tongue, use it wisely. Let
the words of God be your words. Tell your body what the Lord has promised you, and you will walk in His love, peace, and joy in a strong and
healthy body.

CLOSE ATTENTION

I have for you today a word of great importance requiring your close
attention. Do not doubt or consider that this is not just for YOU! When I
bring a word it is only for your good, but this word is more important than

that. How long do you really think you have before I catch you away? This question is one requiring primary focus because your time is now so limited! Every hour you have should be directed toward your Spiritual growth and the salvation of the lost. Do not continue in worthless endeavors, but spend your time drawing My words into your heart, learn obedience from all you do! Be obedient to My call on your life. I have eternal blessings all set for those who read and do! Now review what here is written and grow from its urgency.

Be aware of and recognize Me, the Holy Spirit within you. I am your helper, your teacher, and your comforter. God has granted you His power and blessings through Me, as I am a part of the Godhead. Know that I am here to teach you what God wants you to know for I have all truth from God. Let My Spirit become one with your Spirit and We can direct the soul and body. The blessings I have for you will make your life complete and you will have life abundantly. Look to Me for peace, love and joy, for goodness, faith and patience. These blessings are promised to you in the word and together We will make them a part of your life. Walk in obedience to the word and be led by your friend the Holy Spirit, and you will receive the crown of life promised by God.

WALKING THE WALK

There are times when you and I must see eye to eye. Times of loving, times of witnessing, times of danger, all of these have a purpose of welding Our Oneness. Never think your day-by-day time is wasted, keep your eyes on me, keep your thoughts on me, and keep your heart close to My heart all of the time. These last days have great importance and great compensation to all of My loved ones who are walking the walk and talking the talk that demonstrates My love. Keep drawing Me closer every day now because of the nearness of departure. Only the Father knows when, but We all know how, The Great Catching Away, and what a time that will be!

My child walk boldly and in peace each day. You are going forward, just take baby steps toward Me, having confidence that I am with you, My love is sustaining you, and the Holy Spirit is leading the way. Meditate and focus on your Heavenly Father, remember He is Almighty God. He is drawing you to Himself as you seek His peace. Forget self and the things of the world, and move upward ever mindful of His support and love. Create an atmosphere of love about you. Draw others into this circle of God's love. Let them see Jesus in you. Jesus is the way, the truth, and the life. Persevere, My love will show the way.

SONSHINE OF VICTORY

Into every life must flow setbacks and upsets, these are but foundation stones of worth to be built upon. Take each time of sorrow and setback as a well of understanding, and draw from it wisdom and guidance for future use. Always look upon your troubles as necessary experiences of learning, believe these are useful to your molding and fashioning into the child I am drawing you to be. Never consider that you are alone in tragedy, but make of each undesirable occasion a time of Our relationship. I am always with you, but to make My presence known in times of trouble is to receive unexpected blessings in new ways. Always look for the Sonshine of Victory in each occasion. All My loved ones are not on a downward path, but on an uplifting in every way. Draw on your breath from heaven and find the truth of My presence.

God is love, God is a God of mercy, and He knows all and wants His children to know Him. He has prepared a place for His children to be with Him. This earthly time is a learning time. A time to accept and know Jesus, the Son of God, a time to know the word of God and live it. It is a time to love God and to love others. This is the season of lessons and Spiritual growth. Persevere in all situations, showing forth love and understanding. Be the over-comer God intends you to be. He is with you and will lift you up when you call on Him. He is your peace, your strength, and your joy and will see you through. He will direct your path if you lean on Him.

THE TRUE WALK

In every life I can bring relief and physical blessings, sometimes I start there, and I can continue because of their reception, and carry them into Spiritual blessings. The true walk is to grow Spiritually, but that seems to be a wall that few penetrate. My dear ones learn this lesson today because it carries great worth to the obedient ones. Control your physical walk by allowing My Spirit to guide you, and then you will find your Spiritual opportunities opening up. Only by reading My Bible and learning self-control will your walk grow. My word is your guide, your counselor, and your constant help, My Spirit is your guide and helper in all you do. I am always a present help also, so call on Me, and know the Father is always watching with great care. What kind of a picture is this that I'm giving you? You are surrounded with loving care, can't you see, feel, trust, and know it?

You are the temple of the Holy Spirit, and you have all the power within you that raised Jesus Christ from the dead. Call on this power and I, the Holy Spirit, will lift you up. I have blessings from the Father for you, blessings that will enable you to live an abundant life. You have things to do for the Father. Be the light in your dark world. Show forth Jesus to all others. Let God's presence enfold you with love, peace, and joy, and then give this to others. Grow more like Jesus every day, and be compassionate, loving, and caring. "Your God shall supply all your needs according to his riches in Glory through Jesus Christ." Walk confidently, knowing that you are able to do God's work in love and peace. Together We can do all things!

CLOSE ATTENTION

Never is there a time that I am not watching over My children. Every child of Mine has that close attention needed to draw him along. This attention is given especially when My child is aware of and enjoying the comfort I give. All things grow into wonder and blessings when they are as close to Me as I am to them. This is the climax of purpose, mutual love given freely. What a time of warmth and growth when We can be of one-way, one path, one direction all from the Father of All. Keep Our Oneness growing because there is no better goal to be attained. Make your walk My way for you, and We will have a wonderful victory in Our Oneness.

"Trust in the Lord with all your heart, lean not on your own understanding. In all you ways acknowledge Him and He will direct your path." Keep God's word always foremost in your mind. In His word comes the power, the guidance, and the peace needed to overcome in this world.

Trust that all things, all your needs, are being supplied as you walk hand in hand with the Heavenly Father. His love covers you as a shield, bringing forth protection, health, peace, guidance, and most of all, the Glory of His love. Have a heart of thanksgiving for you are a blessed child of God. His love will see you through.

A DAILY PATH

The things of worth that are before you each day will only help you when you acknowledge, see, know, and perform them to the best of your ability. Call on Me I will answer your whys and hows when you make Me a part of the things you do daily, and you will find excellence and confidence pursuing you. Come let us walk a daily path of Oneness in all you do and your Spiritual growth will thrive. Your walk in My hands is a path of victory over all that comes your way. Let My Spirit lead you in your path of righteousness.

It is the time to walk in peace. Rest in the Lord and lean on His everlasting arms. Let your Heavenly Father direct your ways. He is with you, He is within you, you are One with your Lord, so acknowledge Him and let Him show the way. The word says, "I am the way, the life force, your peace, and your daily walk." There is comfort in knowing you are not alone. He is the God of your spirit, soul, and body. Submit self and walk in Glory with your loving Father.

THE BIG VIEW

The continuing of your work must go on, and it is good that you know this. Every effort in the pursuit of what My will for you is will generate great rewards and benefits to many, not only to yourself. To be able to continue in My work will only become easier as it becomes more regular and right. Stay on the course I set, do not deviate because it will only result in slow downs and loss, not only to you but many others. It is important to see the big view of what you are doing. Never look upon your reading as a small or useless thing because it is of Me, for Me, and with Me. Keep your eyes more and more on Our purposes and your purpose will become quite evidential, stay the course and draw closer day by day. Yes claim your victories and I will have more to work with!

SHOW ME

In every hour of the day, I give My children opportunities to know Me. To know Me in others, to know me in the trees and shrubs, to know Me in the sky and heavens. Why is it My children don't know Me better? Come My dear ones, you who do call on Me and do know Me, can't you tell the lost ones about Me and show Me through your works? Haven't I tried to lead you? Don't you feel the tug on your heart when the lost ones are near? Come, I will lead you, I will guide you, I will give you the right time and words to use. Just let go of self and draw closer to Me daily, and We will finish the work the Father has given Us.

Your body is the temple of the Holy Spirit. You are filled with His power, love, and peace. You can have the abundant life God promised in His word by releasing these blessings. Set self aside and permit the Holy Spirit to become real to you. Walk daily in God's presence. Have a thankful heart, for you know that God is your only source of all things. Focus on Jesus Christ, truly your example, as well as your Lord and Savior. His great sacrifice made all things possible for you. His love will lift you over the trials and tribulations of life. Because of Him you are an over-comer. Walk in this love and you will be a blessing.

THE WORDS

All the words I bring to My children are but help to those who use them. Words written or spoken are only on paper that disappears, or in the air that dissipates. Think about the use you make of the words I give you. If you speak My words in truth, force, and belief they can heal, cleanse, and keep you, but if they are spoken only to hear the sound, the worth flies away never to help anyone. Think more about what has just been written, bury it in your heart, use it and great will be your benefits. I give you many words, over and over again; do they just fly by you? What worth are My words spoken to you in sincerity and love?

God is in His heaven; all is well with the earth. He is watching over all His children, supplying what is needed, bringing peace where there is turmoil and strengthening the weak. His great desire is for all to know Him and to grow Spiritually. He would that you walk in His presence always. For in His presence is fullness of joy. Be led by the Holy Spirit and you will stay in His presence. Walk in peace with a heart full of love and thanksgiving. Let God's love be manifested in your life so that others may know you are a child of God. Live the abundant life God has planned for you. "Put on the garment of praise for the spirit of heaviness," for I am with you.

NEVER CEASE

The continuing pursuit of My way for you will pay off in great rewards. But the pursuit that pleases Me is the one that never stops, never hesitates, and is always truth seeking. This task, once begun, should never cease because what or where else would you go? Only self-pleasing or man-pleasing can be the other choice, has either of those ever paid a positive, long-lasting dividend? Clear thinking only comes from a clear conscience, and I am the only source of that. With Me comes freedom of self and pursuit of true love. I am the pivot-point of all true love; only My love carries long lasting assurances of peace and comfort. Take the time you still have left to sit in the silence of My presence and wait upon Me. Only by your time given to Me can you draw from My well of happiness. Only by this method can I give truth the time and place you need to grow.

Always pray to your Heavenly Father in the name of Jesus. Use the name of Jesus regularly to bring His presence into your life. It is your faith in Jesus that makes you a part of the family of God. Jesus' great love and sacrifice made it possible for you to know God as your Father. You have become joint-heirs with Jesus through His love for you. The way has been made; it is for you but to walk in it. "Jesus is the way, the truth and the life." Walk in His way, know truth through Him, and let His life shine through you.

PART OF THE VICTORY

If every day each of My children would follow My Holy Spirit's leading I would soon have Our Meeting in the Clouds. Father God has set a number for His Family and He will not change it. Only when His Family is complete will I be allowed to bring Our meeting in the air together. So dear ones, who read and understand this word you, each one, are to be looked upon as part of the victory. How soon is still in the making, but dear ones for everyone you bring to the saving knowledge of Jesus Our time grows shorter. Isn't this incentive enough to motivate you to be My witnesses daily? Come let Us gather Our Family NOW!

Walk in love at all times. Look around you and see what others need. See a need and fill it. To love others is the most important thing you have to do, after loving God. Let go of self, and let God have His way in you. His way is one of love. This time on earth is the time to learn to love. You are to love others as God has loved you. Spend time showing God's love to others. Let God's peace permeate your heart and soul. See others with the eyes of Jesus, focusing on the good and not the negative. Allow God's light to shine on others and the darkness will flee. Receive all the love God has for you, walk in His presence, and let this be a river of love flowing out from you.

WHO I AM

There are very few children doing everything I ask, and fewer still doing anything I ask, how much I appreciate those who do listen for My words and then do them. Keep up the listening, and hearing with actions and doing, this is your road to victory and brings victory within the reach of many children. Never put down or fail to appreciate the words I give you. I do not throw My words around carelessly or without thought and purpose. Keep in mind who I am that's talking to you and show proper respect always. We are friends and growing into much more than that so give all I say proper regard. I only pour out My loving care with careful regard to who and where it goes. No move I make is wasted and should never be put aside as useless. Watch over and give proper regard to all that I bring to you, and great results will be the reward for all involved.

Walk uprightly with your head lifted toward heaven for there, in the Almighty God, is your source. Use what you have now doing God's work, always confident that your Heavenly Father, "Will supply all your needs according to His riches in Glory through Jesus Christ," this also applies to your health. Rise, depending on God to supply your strength and your health each day. Jesus took your infirmities and diseases on Himself so you could be free of the curse. Walk in this freedom. Claim the abundant life Jesus came to give you. You are a child of the living God, joint-heirs with Jesus. Walk in and claim the way that He made for you. Go forth in His presence and fulfill the purpose He created you for, you are able for the Holy Spirit leads you.

ONLY TRUTH

The feelings of man basically exhibits the flesh of man, My dear children do not be led by your feelings but be led by My Spirit. How you ask? Just trust and believe when We talk together about your questions that I will submit to you only truth. It is through Our discussions you will be fed truth for your walk each day. It is most important that you and I talk every morning, how else will you know My path for you? When My child follows My Holy Spirit's leading then truth's banner is flying for all men to see. It is not appropriate for My children to follow self and or self-pleasing ways. Take great care about this from now on because then I can use you more appropriately. Your growth will carry you to great heights of service for the Kingdom, not much is said about My Kingdom but that is where all My children will live eternally so set your hearts to be Kingdom pleasers!

Let the Lord set the pace in your life, do not hurry or be a sluggard. Walk and live in the flow of life that has been established by your Heavenly Father. There is a time to work and a time to rest. It is advantageous to wait upon the Lord for then your strength will be renewed. Remember to lean on Him for your well being is through Him. "The joy of the Lord is your strength." Let His joy bubble up in your soul and it will restore your being. My child, I have planned an abundant life for you. Walk in My way, the path I have prepared for you, and you will enjoy abundance every day of your life.

SEEKING ME

There are many children seeking a closer walk with Me, but they are inconsistent in their efforts. This shall no longer be! Your time isn't long enough for further procrastination. Now is all the time you have left, there will not be "sometime later." Come My dear ones and rise early in the morning, seeking Me in the quiet. I am always there waiting. I have great and wonderful things to tell you. Where you are going, how you'll get there, what you'll be doing at arrival. I'm not a God of mysteries but of revelation. Come listen, hear Me, learn more of Me, and how I love you. Find your place in My plan. Learn to walk the walk you've been made for. All this will occur at your obedient attention. Tell Me, why do you hesitate?

My word to you is life for your body and direction for your life. If you submit to and obey My word you will be kept in My presence, protected, lifted up and shown the way. Jesus made the way, opened the door to heaven and the presence of God. The word [The Bible] was given to show the way daily, step by step, as you go through this life. Jesus is your example. He is Holy as God is Holy. In Him is all of God's righteousness. Fashion your life in His image. Walk in love as He did, exhibit the fruit of the Holy Spirit such as patience, love, joy self-control, faith, meekness, and gentleness. Be always led by the Holy Spirit knowing that your Heavenly Father is with you. Rejoice for you have been chosen to be a member of God's Family!

MOST NEGLECTED

The most important things of life seem to be the most neglected things of My children. Why is man's life so filled with useless clutter day after day? To walk and talk with Me daily should be your first priority, why isn't it? I left you in charge of your life because I only wanted the children who truly loved Me to be My family, but all those I chose seem so reluctant to run after and seek My will and way daily. This is a wake- up call to all who will listen. Don't follow self any longer, My soon return is too important for you to miss. Start new with Me each day, then I can draw you into your planned place of forever because I love you. This is a sure wake-up call!

God allows circumstances to come into your life so you will grow Spiritually. When all is rosy you are not challenged to seek out God and His solutions to your problems. Can you act in a Godly manner when trials and tribulations have come upon you? At a time like that can you be submissive and let God lead you out of the situation? It is a time of testing your faith. Can you walk in righteousness when evil is trying to overcome you? God is your protection, your shield, and your defense against evil. Wrap yourself in the presence of the Lord. Be confident that He is with you always. His love is your protection, rest in it!

MINE FOREVER

When I call a child to be Mine it is an everlasting call, they are to be Mine Forever! My children, do not fail to grasp what has just been said, it implies eternity, always and forever, only Gods last that long. You are Forever Family. Never has such a thing been done before like I am doing on this earth with My chosen ones. Do not take this position that I am extending so lightly! I am very serious about this Family Thing, and I expect you to be also! This is straight talk and I am expecting 100% compliance. Make this day a new commitment that My time is all the time you have, because Our time is Forever. Start fresh this day and walk, and talk, and in every thing you do acknowledge Me as being right there with you. It is so, and more so as you make it!

In the name of Jesus make all your requests known to the Father. Jesus tells us "Whatever you ask the Father in My name He will give you." That name carries the authority and power of God Almighty. Use that name as a covering of protection, and as a source of strength. It will bring a river of peace into your life. You are joint-heirs with Jesus Christ so claim what you have been promised. When the worries of the world and self overcome you, whisper that name "Jesus." Self and the world will fade away as Jesus becomes uppermost in your thinking. When darkness comes upon you dispel it with the light that is in Jesus' name. He is your source call on Him. Rejoice for you are a child of the living God!

GREAT TRUTHS

The things of the world are fading away for My children as I bring truth and life abundant to My loved ones. Time not only changes but time also fades away. This note is a wake-up call for My listening ones, your time on this earth, the way it is and the way that it's becoming, is fast changing to fulfill My purposes. The time for preparation for abandonment is here, and those who listen now will benefit the most. Yes dear ones you are to leave this place shortly because this earth is not for you during this time coming. I have not held you close to bring these changes to you; I've held you close to save you from the things to come. Hear this word for it is salvation to your body, soul, and spirit. Pay heed to what is said, I've shown it all to you in the Bible and now great truths are about to flow.

This message is from Me, the Holy Spirit within you. I bring to you the life force from God, your Heavenly Father. In Me is the power, the love, and peace of God. I have for you Godly wisdom if you will but call on Me and receive it. I am truth as He is truth. Those that are led by My voice are truly the sons of God. Listen for My still soft voice, dear one, and receive all the Father has for you. He has planned a life of abundance for you. I am the power that raised Jesus from the dead, and the Father loves you so much that He sent that power to indwell you. Set self aside and walk the path He has prepared for you. I am here for your Spiritual growth unto righteousness. Let Me show the way to your perfection. "To be Spiritually minded is life and peace."

WORK OF PREPARING

When I desire to bless My children I quicken My word in their hearts. Many children have I blessed in this manner, but many do not use or follow through with My urgings. Why is that? Self leads the basic nature of man, "I want to do it Myself," or "I can do it Myself." When this response occurs I must back off, only when they ask for and then receive My help by their obedience, can I help them. Dear ones this is not the time to be acting like that. We have a work of preparing Jesus' Bride and only by receiving My help can this Bride be prepared, WHO YOU ARE! Come now submit to My word, the Bible, as never before because there has never before been a time with Me such as you are having right now. Grow from just trying to really doing all that I ask. It is all for your blessing, believe and receive all you can conceive.

Receiving and releasing love in your life loosens the power of God. God is love! All real love comes from Him. He wants it spread around the world by His children. The love of God is the light and dispels the darkness, or evil. When there is light there cannot be darkness. Choose thoughts of love, of God's love. "God so loved the world, [you] that He gave His only Son." See others through the eyes of love, as Jesus sees them. Focus on the good, the positive, the lovely, and the worldly evil will fade away. Jesus commands, "That ye love one another, as I have loved you." In this manner righteousness will come forth and you will have fullness of joy!

HEART'S DESIRE

There are many ways for My children to draw closer to Me, but when they have a strong desire in their heart that won't be denied, then I am most pleased. When your heart's desire is for a closer walk you have just opened up Our best walk together that anyone can have. Some children come quickly into this way of love but most take quite a while because of a strong self. This note today is to tell all who read and heed, there is not much time to continue to please self and still be My saved one. Come now dear ones hear these warnings I give to you in many ways because of the urgency of the times. Do not neglect to gather yourselves together in fellowship with Me, also do not forsake Our individual walk daily. Our closeness, your obedience, and loves walk will pave your path with victory to be enjoyed forever!

Almighty God is in charge so rest in Him, waiting upon Him , and He will show the way. He has not planned anything for you that you cannot accomplish. He will make a way. Remember "I can do all things through Christ who strengthens me." This is God's word and promise to you if you stay connected to Him. Walk daily in peace knowing He is directing your path. "He that has begun a good work in you shall perform it." Let His plan mature in your life. As a member of the body of Christ let your part be performed and completed through Jesus.

WORK AND WALK

The daily work and walk of My loved ones are the making and forming of their future place of forever. Yes this little old earth is also the forming environment in which My children of the future become full Sons and Daughters. Take more thought about the what and where of your future, because now you have the irreplaceable opportunity to make a great and worthy place beside Me. The high positions of My Kingdom are places of honor and blessings, and I do not lightly chose who will set in such offices. Take heed of how your heart is developing now because I am watching with great anticipation for your wakening to My call.

Today is a day of restoration. Be restored and renewed through the power and mercy of Almighty God. Walk in the light as He is in the light and let His presence renew your being. Have the mind of Jesus Christ, and let His Glory wash over you. Today receive the wonderful fruit of the Holy Spirit. It is a precious gift to you from God. Let His love become your love, His peace your peace, and truly your joy will be fulfilled. As a child of God all these blessings are for you if you will but overcome the world and self.

"Humble your self in the sight of the Lord and He will lift you up." Walk uprightly in His power and grace that your joy may be complete.

TRUTH AND DEPTH

The meaning of My words in the Bible are only true as I give release for My truth to go forth and do the work I have ordained it should do. Self-pleasers cannot read and do My words in their truth and depth. Only My Spirit can release truth that is from Me. Learn the lesson from this message dear ones, do not take My words lightly for they are part of Me, and I dwell in power behind My words. My power is released through My words so My children can learn to create and operate as I do. I am training My obedient ones to act as I would act and do as I would; behind all this must be My motivating love driving all you do. This is a lesson you must bring to Me and We will open up to you where you are to fit in.

Allow the scriptures to permeate your being. Let God's word become a part of you. The word is health to your body. God's word says "A merry heart doeth good like a medicine." Claim the word of God for your life as these promises are for you, child of God. Have that abundant life the Lord has prepared for you. Eagerly anticipate each day, and face it with an attitude of peace and joy as you look forward to what God will do in your life today. Use each situation as a source, a learning experience to grow Spiritually, and your joy will flood your soul.

BRING THEM HOME

There is a never- ending need for My children to call out to My lost ones and bring them home. Yes home with Me, I desire My whole family complete and with Me, this is My purpose and plan. You who know Me are My source of salvation for My lost ones and I call again to save My lost children! Tell them I love them; tell them I'm coming soon, very very soon. Come now you who read this, and hear Me in your heart, the time for "Wrap-up" is nearing and almost here. No longer drag your feet in hesitation and doubt but speak up, call out, reach out, and touch My lost children their time is now and you are My tools and source for their salvation. Make a new brother or sister in the Lord this day, which is My call to you!

Think joy and happiness today. Remember the promises in the word to you. Rejoice for your Heavenly Father is always with you .You are strengthened by this attitude, "The joy of the Lord is my strength," Call on this strength and joy to do the will of the Father. Extend your hand in mercy and love to all others, and then you will be God's extended hand. Let peace flood your soul. God promises "My peace I give you, not as the world gives, give I to you." Receive this glorious peace. It will renew your life and make Spiritual growth more easily attained. Rest in Him, wait upon Him, and enjoy the abundant life He has for you.

NEWER LIFE

There are many ways My children can go that please Me, but the way that pleases Me the most is following My Holy Spirit's leading. This simple action will bring each obedient one into a closer walk with Me daily, and We will find a newer life living closer to each other. This is the desire of My heart. Why can't it become your desire too? Spend each morning with Me, and then We can walk a daily walk of friendship and pleasure in all We do. Come dear ones your time pleasing self must come to its end, and your walk forever with Me must take place. Why are you looking back to do the old things each day when I can bring you into a walk of pleasant joy and happiness. I have no other plans than to draw you into a closer eternal friendship starting today!

Rejoice, for you have another day to do the work God has created you to do. Thank God for His many blessings in your life. Go forth and share these blessings with the lost ones, and with the family of God. Let God's light be reflected in you, My child. Let His Glory and love show in your life. Love the unlovely, those in darkness, they too are My children and need My love. Bring light and love into this dark world. I am coming soon, help in the gathering, for soon it will be too late. It is truly harvest time. As a joint-heir with Jesus, spread God's love; and let all hear the message of salvation. Be an active member of the body of Christ. Do all in love and My joy will be your covering.

ASK BELIEVING

Many are My children who do right, seek right, and long to be right; they have already their hope in the future in their hearts and life now. I draw every child of Mine into their place with Me as soon as they ask, believing. When their belief equals their desire I am there executing their way with all My blessings. Few children will so commit but commit they must. Our relationship throughout eternity must have the sealed perfection of Christ dwelling in them forever. This note is guidance for the believing, willing ones. Is this you today? Do you really have this full heart commitment so strong that Jesus can abide with you forever? Come dear ones this is the path to Glory. Forever, make it positive this day in your heart; say, "Jesus is in My heart Forever, and Ever and Ever. Amen."

Replace all negative and critical thoughts with thoughts of Jesus and His word and His love. This will restore the light to your soul. The Bible asks God's children to "Have the mind of Christ." By doing this you are blocking out the evil of self and the world. The heart of man is wicked, but you have the indwelling Holy Spirit to lead the way, this includes your thought life. "May the words of my mouth and the meditations of My heart be acceptable in thy sight, Oh Lord my strength and my redeemer." Let David's prayer in the Psalms be your prayer.

THE IMAGE

With continuing service in obedience to My Holy Spirit in you, I can lift you closer and closer to the image of My Son Jesus. This dear children is the everlasting path to victory in this world. Assurance will become your badge of blessings and you will walk in newness of Spirit every day. This is the path of sure victory for every dear soul who is led daily by My Holy Spirit. Keep yourself close by your daily talk and walk with Me. Never neglecting the things that I have told you will strengthen and straighten your path each step you take. Know that I am ever watching over you with loving actions of blessings as you follow in all I show you. Stay the course shown to you, and your climb into your place with Me will be assured.

Remember the power that raised Jesus from the dead dwells within you. It is in the Holy Spirit, the gift God gave you when you accepted Jesus as your Lord and Savior. Call on this power, this strength and wisdom daily as needed. It was given to you to be used, to be a blessing in your life. The fruit of the Holy Spirit is to help you in your Spiritual growth. Call upon the patience, self-control and gentleness that is yours through the Holy Spirit. Claim the love, peace and joy available to you and see your faith grow. Trust that these blessings are yours but must be received; they must be loosed into your life to be effective. Grow daily in your Spiritual life by drawing on the blessings and power of the Holy Spirit. Go from Glory to Glory in your walk toward your Heavenly Father.

HEAR THIS

There will be a continuing pressure put on all of My children of obedience, because the shortage of time demands the work of the Father shall be done. Hear this message all My children, because it is your answer to the happenings occurring around you. Rush and pressure seem required to keep My working ones pursuing the tasks I require them to do. Let no slip-up occur to disrupt the timing and tempo of things the Father has set in motion. These are the most important "wrap-up" tasks of the body of Christ that the Father requires. No one left out, no one left behind, then no one will be blamed for loses occurring. All of the planned blessings from the Father will roll on in increasing frequency, bringing the joy that has been set for all of God's children to see how the Father is viewing the events of this time. Come see all occurrences, for these times, as from the Father's heart.

Jesus is the Lord and Savior for all mankind, from the beginning to the end of the world. All men have the choice to believe that Jesus is the Son of God and accept Him as Lord and Savior or to reject Him. God has given His children free will to make this choice. You have a lifetime to make this decision and then live a life of growing righteousness. After you choose Jesus you have the Holy Spirit indwelling to lead and guide you in the path God has prepared for you. You are covered by the presence and love of God in your daily walk. Search out the directions for your life in the Word, Lean on Him for He cares for you. Give praise and thanksgiving for the joy of being a child of God. Now walk in an abundant life!

MOVING EVENTS

There is about to break forth a great display by the Father of Heavenly wonders for His children to observe. Do not miss what is here said because it is a forerunner of moving events calling forth the children of obedience to a new level of understanding. Look for and be aware that this is coming for all the children of the earth. No group will be overlooked. This will be a first "Wake up" call to the whole earth for God's children to know that He is real and is sending Jesus for the greatest gathering of saved ones that has ever occurred or will ever occur! The word of God is to be made alive in sight and truth before all to see and then will come the final harvest so longed for by Father God. Gather My lost ones, tell them Jesus loves them, and is coming at last for all who hear and answer this call.

Be strong, knowing that the Holy Spirit within will lead you in the right path. Be confident, knowing anything God has for you to do He will make a way. Remember, "the joy of the Lord is your strength." Have a heart of praise and worship, along with joy, and your strength will be renewed. When all seems overwhelming wait on the Lord and He will renew your strength, you are the temple of the Holy Spirit. The almighty power of God resides in you and for you. Release this power in your life, acknowledge it and call upon it. It is God's gift to you. Submit yourself to God and receive all He has for you.

ALL IS WELL

The things I am giving in these books belong to all of My children, but it takes all of Our cooperation to bring it about. Do not be discouraged Our plan is unfolding and I am moving events in place for the release We are all waiting for. Just keep on reading as you are and We will all be blessed at the results that will occur. Our words are precious and worth great effort to support so don't slack off or be slow in finishing what is given you. Keep your eyes on the daily task and I will be setting future events in proper perspective. By studying these words you are building a fine inheritance for all who will receive what We are doing. Just know all is well!

"Arise and shine, for the Glory of the Lord is upon you." Imagine the Glory of the Lord being upon you! In God's Glory are love, power, strength, wisdom, and peace. All of these blessings and more are covering you, and are available to you if you will but receive. Take hold of what God has for you, His child. To receive focus on the Lord, give praise and worship so that thoughts of self will be eliminated as you bathe in His love. Let the mind of Christ Jesus be in you as you direct all thoughts of God in worship of Him. "Be still and know that I am God." These are His directions to the body of Christ. Still self and receive His Glory, with it comes an abundant life. Rejoice in Him.

HIGH PLACES

Everything the world has to offer you is not what I desire, stop listening to the world and start listening all of the time you have left to Me. I am calling out to all and everyone who will listen and do, not just listeners but doers! Only the obedient will be lifted up to the high places in My time. Just turn around everything the world has to offer you now for Satan and his minions are moving as never before, they think it is their time to rule and reign, but I am only allowing them to express the things I will allow, I'm still the patient overseer. Watch carefully the times that are before you because I am shaping them to conform to My plan. Don't get caught up on the wrong side of this effort. Call on Me and seek My face and voice as never before. The time of pleasant playing is fast turning into the wonderful times of everlasting decision-making.

Allow God to use you in His plan. His plan is harvest, the time of the gathering of all His sheep into His Kingdom. God's saved children are the ones to send forth the salvation message to let the whole world know about Jesus and His love. Will you be a part of this plan? Listen for the directions from the Holy Spirit, God's voice to you. He created you for such a time as this, to be a willing worker with a desire to see the lost ones saved. Draw close to the Lord in prayer as you bring the lost before the Savior. Have a heart of compassion for God's children in darkness. Be a bearer of light and brighten the lives of those who do not know Jesus. Be an extension of Jesus today and bring joy to others.

ALL NEW

New ways, new times, new experiences, all new blessings flowing in quantities never before seen, yes there is coming a breakthrough of mighty proportions showing the lost My power and love. Waiting is about over, hoping is to be dashed as hope's dreams come forth. The sights and sounds of My heaven's release will stir and awaken this earth into a revival such as has never been. Thousands and thousands coming to the Lord as never before, gifts flowing, dreams appearing in reality, blessings overflowing, and the earth rejoicing in new ways. Yes new children receiving Christ as Savior as never before, the flood breaks forth, the children saved, the healings flow, and there will be sights and sounds of newness from heaven. Pray My children, pray My listening ones, pray all who know Me, pray as never before, and I will hear and answer from heaven with an earth resounding like never before and never again. Yes, I'll hear from heaven and send the release, I will, I *will!*

"My peace I give you, not as the world gives, give I to you. Let not your heart be troubled," this is God's word to you. Rest in this peace; let the worldly cares slip away in this peace. It is through God's peace that understanding comes, that strength is renewed. Your health and well-being depend on you abiding in His peace. Connect with the Lord constantly in prayer, worship, praise, and reading the word. For it is in this connection that peace comes. Let your mind be filled with Godly thoughts, thoughts that are pure, lovely, honest, true, and not negative but uplifting. This will determine your attitude and give you joy as you please the Lord.

YOUR PART

There are times of trouble, times of sorrow, times of failures, and upsetting occurrences, these are only My hand fashioning you into the Christ like self that I seek. It is your part to give thanks in everything because you love and trust Me. If I can't have a proper response, then We must come again together in other ways until your awareness reaches My desire. My dear ones you are part of a host of wonder works of Mine bringing into being a family of forever for My Kingdom. How I form it, how I love it, how I draw, change, and alter it, should only bring forth thanks and understanding, because I have not hidden Myself completely. The eyes that are opened will experience growth and works that produce blessings for evermore, so take this note as a sweet pill and swallow it with joy and understanding, because then I will see your growth and reward you greatly!

"He which has begun a good work in you will perform it until the day of Jesus Christ." God's word, His promise to you, is a source of joy knowing He has a purpose for your life and He is performing it. Are you going to be a hindrance or help? Are you learning the lessons from each trial and stumbling block in your life? God's wish is that you go from Glory to Glory in your Spiritual growth. Step up and rise above the level you are now on. Step out knowing you are not alone. God is supplying all your needs and leading the way. He will not put upon you more than you are able to handle. Step out in confidence that whatever you are going through is a lesson learned with Jesus by your side!

REAL GROWTH

When I desire to reveal new wonders and blessings to My children I do not wait until they are perfect and right in all of their ways, no My love flows over and above such minor obstacles. My love is forever love and loving, My desires are the ways of perfection, and all who support My desires finds new blessings every day. If you give thanks for only the big things of worth that occur to you, you will be missing the long sustaining support of moment by moment small blessings. Give thanks for all things because that brings a joy to My heart. It means you are more aware of My constant care over you in everything. When you walk in awareness of Me all the time, giving Me credit for everything in your life, then you are walking in the reality of truth; this is real growth in the Spirit!

Have a heart full of love, and let it shine through you in your daily life. Without love as the motivator all activity is useless to the Father. Examine self and see why you are doing what you are doing. You have been commanded to love one another. This truly is the will of God for your life, to love God and to love one another. Many little things done in love are stepping-stones to a closer walk with the Lord. Determine to make your will the Father's will for you. Receive the great love He has for you, and reflect it on everyone you meet. This attitude will subdue self and allow the righteousness of God to fill your being.

CALL ON ME

There are many forces moving in this world and I am aware of every one of them. When you have problems call on Me and I will answer. It is this use of Me that draws Us closer together every day. My dear children I'm showing you your path to eternity by drawing you into all of the ways I help and teach you. Unless We are together in everything you do We are not working as We should. Stop your practice of "I'll do it myself" and to say We'll do it together. Call on Me all of the time, not some of the time, because this is your path to victory over self and the world! The time is now for your permanant turn around, begin to walk a closer walk now!

Allow the presence of God to penetrate your being. Receive the love and the blessings He has for you. Take of the healing power bestowed upon you by Jesus Christ for "By His stripes you were healed." Infirmity, sickness and pain have no right in your body because Jesus took all of that upon His body. My children, receive the blessings, learn the lessons, and persevere always under trial and tribulation, for this is a learning time, a growing time in the Spirit. The Father has great rewards for you if you stay the course. His love and power will see you through. Keep your eyes on Jesus. Go forth boldly knowing He is always with you.

A RECEPTIVE HEART

When there is a receptive heart then I can fill out My plan for that one. I never stop desiring more and better for each child of Mine. When you are Mine you give Me all the time I need with you, to lift you up in the Spirit, to show you how to live in the flesh, to bring you guidance and teachings, as you need them. All My intentions and desires are for nothing when you do not give Me time with you each day. Until I am "All you time" you will never receive "All your blessings." Your greatest task now is to be still and know what I am saying is truth to follow. What is more important to you after I tell you Our time together like this, now, is fast coming to an end? Then much of your way will be set and your walk will be different than the one We are sharing at this time. Take full advantage of each day to bring forth the reality of what I say in this note today.

"This is the day the Lord has made. I will rejoice and be glad in it." Be thankful today for the many blessings in your life. Focus on Jesus and His love, and His sacrifice for the children of God. With a heart full of thanksgiving go forth showing God's love. Let that light shine in you that is the love of God. Be aware of God's Glories about you. See everything and everyone with the eyes of Jesus. Acknowledge that God is your source of all things and praise and worship will bubble up in your heart. Give thanks this day because you have been chosen, and you are a child of the most High God!

WALK TOGETHER

There will never a perfect time for My children to find eternal life, because I have the scenes required for every child to have the same opportunity in different times and different places to find the path of eternal salvation. I watch over all equally, and I expect only My called ones to be saved. Yes, I call every child of Mine, and everyone will respond sufficiently for Me to save and draw him or her closer to Me. Our walk is a "Walk Together" or it is no walk at all. Every lesson I give has a person's name attached to it. I create every way I can to save the lost ones, each salvation is a timed and known event, planned and moved at My direction. Only obedient children led by My Spirit are the chosen of My salvation for the lost. Obedience is the key to My strategies and obedience from and through love is the only way. Keep this lesson in mind, and seek always to be led by My Spirit.

Let your faith rise to cover all you are praying for. "The effectual fervent prayer of a righteous man availith much." This is My word and promise to you. When you pray, ask believing and it will be done for you. Your heavenly Father sends ministering spirits [angels] to minister to the heirs of salvation. It is important to pray in God's will, and it will come to pass. Pray for God's will in your life, and then follow the leading of the Holy Spirit. The Holy Spirit is all of God, His wisdom, peace, and His power is within you waiting to be released into your life. His love covers you at all times. Be aware of the blessings that are yours, and walk in them for God truly loves you!

OUR WALK

It is with great joy I bring the daily word to you, because as you read, study, believe, and do I can be blessed with each of your efforts. Do not think dear ones that I miss any of your prayers or loving ways to My children. Keep Me close always, and then I can lead, guide, and protect you. This is the way of Our walk together for these times. Take great care with your walk each day and know it is leading you into My planned place for you where blessing flow all of the time. No time is to be wasted, it is too precious in these last times, so keep Me close and listen and obey. Encourage all My children to listen and hear My voice because it is the planned way of proper growth at this time. Be bold and I will support you, tell the lost I love them.

"Blessed is the man who perseveres under trial, because when he has stood the test he will receive the crown of life that God has promised to those who love Him." These are God's words to His chosen ones. Receive the strength and the peace God has for you. Wait upon the Lord with patience because His way and His time are right for you. Cast your cares and burdens on Him for He cares for you. You can do all things through Christ who strengthens you. Let your faith grow, as you trust in your Lord. He will see you through. Have peace in your heart and walk with Him and your joy will be complete.

PLEASE ME

There are many children and I love them all, I show no partiality to any. All, each and every one I love, because My Son has paid dearly for them. So My children heed the words of this book as you would My Bible for I have put My heart and My desires before you plainly, that you may please Me, and so please yourself. Take these books not lightly, because they are your pathways to a closer walk with Me. All who read, understand, obey and do, will find great blessings and rewards forever more. My promises are true and forever. It is to your eternal benefit to believe, your walk will be assured as you read, believe, and do all that is here written. You who are Mine will know in your heart when truth is told. Stand up now and declare that I am God and you are My children!

Let that precious love and peace flow to you from the Heavenly Father. Rest in Him, wait upon Him and receive all the blessings He has for you. His will is that you prosper and be in good health, so go forth confident-ly letting His will and way be manifested in your life. The time is short, allow God to use you to do His will during this time. Remember, "It is all about Jesus." Show your love and desire to please in praise and worship and heart-felt prayers. Listen for directions from Me [Holy Spirit] that the Father's work will be accomplished. Be the child of God you were fash-ioned to be. God is truly in charge and all is well

I am with you now and forever. Lean on Me more; trust Me to help you in all instances. I do hear your prayers; you are so precious to Me, My child. Persevere, you are an over-comer. My love is becoming a part of you. Wait upon Me and together We shall have victory. Be not discour-aged, these lessons are necessary for your Spiritual growth. You are grow-ing daily. Continue to pray for those I put on your heart. Remember your life is like a blue sky, your problems now are just clouds passing by. This too shall pass; My strength is your strength!

COME

When time gets shorter My way is to press harder until all have heard the truth of this word, the place of My family raising. Look all about you, see the times, see the world of man changing, is it for the better or not? My dear ones even the lost know there are great changes in man's activities, and not for the better. I have allowed Satan freedom to move on the hearts of man to test them, this pressure is to make sure who are Mine, and whom he will have. By man's own choice they come with Me or they go to their own place. My challenge to My loved ones is, "Will you help stir and awaken My lost to know Me?" Do not be discouraged, not all are Mine, but you must help weed out the wheat from the chaff. Come all who will, seek to save My children who I am calling. Those who are Mine are One with Me in this effort!

Today is the time to listen to the Holy Spirit and to follow His directions. He has God's plan for you, and He knows the areas in your life that need discipline. When you wait upon the Lord with love in your heart Godly wisdom can be made known to you. Examine yourself and be open to correction. To be led by the Holy Spirit is necessary to please God. Put self aside and let Jesus and His will flood your being. In His love the changes can be made that will draw you into a closer walk with Him. Desire that His will be done in you and through you. This will bring forth the mind and soul of Jesus in you. Oh child of God, submit to the loving correction of your Lord.

TIME OUT

When I move time out of Our way, then your way will be clear. You will see and know in your heart the things that I know in My heart, because We will be One as the Father has ordained. What a time that will be, so My dear ones in light of that coming revelation shouldn't your desire be to know and do faithfully all you can now to bring that about? Study to prove yourself worthy of the calling the Father has put upon you. Open your mind to the things I am saying to you through these books, and look to your growing improvement just as men would look to finding a gold mine. Our walk NOW is the path chosen for all Our loved ones, see that you are walking and talking all the time of Our togetherness, it should be as close as your breath is to your life and living. Awaken to the place you have attained with Us, and rejoice, rejoice, rejoice!

Wait upon the Lord and He shall direct your path. His light will make the way clear. It is a simple walk, one of love, peace and joy as you interact with others. Your attitude reflects what is in your heart. Let your prayer be: "Create in me a clean heart, Oh God, and renew a right spirit within me." This prayer will show your desire to seek first the kingdom of God and His righteousness. God desires for you to have a life of abundance so you can be a blessing to others. Let your light so shine that all may know you are a child of the most High God.

This is only the beginning

The Glories Series
and
Other Books
by
Scott E. Beemer

Studies for Mature Christian Living
BOOK ONE—**SONRISE GLORIES**
Jesus in You
BOOK TWO—**MORNING GLORIES**
Holy Spirit's Morning Journal
BOOK THREE—**ETERNAL GLORIES**
Holy Spirit's Morning Journal
BOOK FOUR—**BELOVED GLORIES**
Holy Spirit's Poems and Proverbs
BOOK FIVE—**LOVABLE GLORIES**
Holy Spirit's Love Notes
BOOK SIX—**GLOWING GLORIES**
Holy Spirit's Journal Notes
BOOK SEVEN—**END TIME GLORIES**
Covenants to Eternity
BOOK EIGHT—**SEEKER'S GLORIES**
Holy Spirit's Seeker's Guide
BOOK NINE—**DYNAMIC GLORIES**
Holy Spirit's Teaching Manual #1
BOOK TEN—**ENDLESS GLORIES**
Holy Spirit's Teaching Manual #2
BOOK ELEVEN—**TRINITY GLORIES**
Holy Spirit's Teaching Manual #3
BOOK TWELVE—**HEAVEN'S GLORIES**
Holy Spirit's Teaching Manual #4
(Last in the Series)

GOD TALK
Beyond Believing, Just Knowing
Love Talk
Volume 1 and 2

You can order these through your favorite bookstore,
or to order direct, contact,

BLACK FOREST PRESS
488 Mountain View Drive
Mosheim, TN 37818
1423-422-4711
You may also order from the shopping cart on Web site
www.mindtreebooks.com

To contact Scott Beemer write to:
GOD'S OPEN FORUM
P.O. Box 80786
San Diego, CA 92138-0786
You may order Scott's Books at this Web site.
www.itsbeensold.com

Printed in the United States
44910LVS00002BA/37-135

Charting a Course for the Church